MERV HUGHES'

104

CRICKET LEGENDS

Other books by this author

Merv Hughes' Best Sporting Insults

MERV HUGHES'
104
CRICKET LEGENDS

Stories, mostly true, about the game's greats

ALLEN&UNWIN
SYDNEY • MELBOURNE • AUCKLAND • LONDON

This edition first published in 2015
First published in 2014

Allen & Unwin
83 Alexander Street
Crows Nest NSW 2065
Australia
Phone: (61 2) 8425 0100
Email: info@allenandunwin.com
Web: www.allenandunwin.com

Cataloguing-in-Publication details are available
from the National Library of Australia
www.trove.nla.gov.au

ISBN 978 1 76029 031 3

Internal design by Squirt Creative
Set in Bitstream Cooper Light by Post Pre-Press Group, Australia
Printed in Australia by McPherson's Printing Group

10 9 8 7 6 5 4 3 2 1

CONTENTS

OPENING THE BOWLING

Tricky word, legend. Could mean a story so fantastic that it is almost unbelievable. A story that is passed down from generation to generation—a bit like stories about cricket and cricketers. Sometimes legend can mean hero. Legend can also be another word for foot.

However you use it, there are more than a hundred legends in this book. Cricketers who *I* think are legends. Who qualify for the title because of what they have done and how they did it and also because of the impact they had on me. I was the 332nd player to play Test cricket for Australia when I made my debut in 1985, 108 years after the first Test match. It is a rare privilege and only happens because of a mixture of many things: accidents of genetics, circumstance, opportunity and luck, most of which are out of the control of the individual. There are many, many players who had the application and the character to make it to a higher level but, for one of these many reasons, couldn't or didn't. That's why I regard a champion as someone who plays the game for the game's sake, who loves the aggression of a competitive situation, who responds positively under pressure and who does everything they can to get the very best out of themselves for the sake of the team. No matter what level they play at. I discovered cricket, learnt how to play the game, played with and against and was taught how to get the best out of myself by the many champions I have met through cricket. These people are my legends.

They all, in some way or another, had an influence on the cricketer that I became. Or they might be the reason I continue to do what I can to stay involved in cricket. Or they might be the other sort of legend: the fantastic story. Some of the stories might even be true.

They say that a batsman can tell you the details of every innings he's played. A bowler can tell you about every wicket he's taken, and every catch dropped by a batsman. Some players can remember a lot of details about the performances of their teammates too, and, sometimes, opponents. When I was thinking about this book, and checking some of my facts, I discovered that some of my memories were indeed very accurate. Checking the statistics also showed me that stats don't always tell the full story. Sometimes they miss almost all of the story. Sure, poor players never have outstanding career numbers. Great players do. But often, players who had a huge impact on their team's performance may not have great figures either: bowlers bowl in pairs; they bowl to instructions; they put pressure on batsmen and others take the wickets. Batsmen make sacrifices too: they set up games by taking risks; bat in various conditions. The numbers don't always tell the story.

That's why I've gathered together these legends. Because of the stories. I played Test cricket for nine years but have spent all of my life learning about cricket. I've been taught by some remarkable people. Teammates, coaches, opponents. Players past and present. Most of them have some common characteristics. A lot of them are good blokes. Many of them you will recognise. And there are many others who aren't included here. But when you pick a side, you can only pick eleven. It's the same with legends: you can only pick 104. So some legends didn't make it. Tommy Stevenson in particular was unlucky. My state coaches Alan Connolly, Keith Stackpole and Ian Redpath all had a huge impact on my thinking about cricket as I tried to make my way at first-class level.

Mum and Dad, who are both very competitive sportspeople, always supported me. Dad was a fiery fast bowler and an obstinate, determined batsman. He was a great teacher because he showed, he didn't tell. From when I was very young he put me into situations where I could watch cricketers train and play. But he was always reluctant to come to the MCG to watch me play. These days, watching my own kids, Maddy, Tim and Scott, play, I get more nervous than when I played. Perhaps that's how it was with Dad. But if ever I was going through a bad patch, he would show me videotapes of my delivery when I was bowling well, and he would identify the technical aspects that had changed for the worse. So he was watching!

This collection is not intended as a statistical reference. I have included career statistics when they illustrate some part of the story. Usually Test and One Day International (ODI) career numbers. Occasionally Twenty20 International figures. For some players, their first-class statistics are more relevant. The format is: number of matches; years of play at that level; runs scored and highest innings; wickets taken and best bowling figures for an innings; number of catches. First-class statistics include Test performances.

PART

1

INSIDE THE DRESSING ROOM

There is no better way to know and understand someone than to play cricket with them. We stand on the paddock, we sit in the rooms waiting to bat, we train, we travel, we eat. Always with our teammates. We plot and celebrate victory. We suffer the anguish of defeat. Watching your teammates prepare for a game, seeing how they react under pressure, helping them battle bad luck and poor form lets you understand them better than anyone else you know. To be given a nickname by the Australian captain is a rare honour. Allan Border christened me Fruit Fly. The great Australian pest. See what I mean?

David Boon

Tests
107 (1984–1996), 7422 runs (200), 99 catches

ODIs
181 (1984–1995), 5964 runs (122), 45 catches

Having played a lot of cricket against David Boon before I got into the Australian team I was always impressed by his strength of character. It didn't matter if it was a green seamer or a flat track, he would just get in behind the ball. I would hit him and hit him and he wouldn't complain, didn't show any pain. He was unflappable. You couldn't flap him. He just had his routine where he would walk down the pitch, tap it, wipe the bottom of the bat, face up, then shuffle his front pad with his left hand. When you played against him you hated it. But when you played with him you just loved it. Watching from the rooms, you were just waiting for it: Oh there it is, mind's on the job.

He was one of the toughest competitors I played with or against. When a side is in trouble, a great player stands up and David Boon did that all the time. Whether it was for Tasmania or for Australia, you knew he was never going to give his wicket away. When we were cruising he cruised a bit but when we were in trouble you could depend on him to be right on his game. He was always the wicket you wanted to get when you played against him. So I always threw everything I had at him, but one thing I didn't do was sledge him.

Sledging means many different things to many different people but in the end it's about bluff and bullshit. You can scare some people and you can bluff some people. I never wasted my breath on Boonie. I recall being in the Victorian room and hearing people discuss whether he was deaf. No one could get anything out of him when he batted.

As a teammate he was strong. A team leader without needing a title. He didn't say much but whatever he did say was always worth taking notice of. I was sitting next to him during a match in Perth against the West Indies waiting to bat in the first innings. Marshall and Ambrose were bowling. I just looked at him and he said, 'Are you scared of fast bowling? Anyone who's not afraid of these fast bowlers isn't all there.'

He told me, 'Some people cope better with fast bowling than others. Just because you're scared doesn't mean you can't cope with it. Go out, watch the ball and you can cope with it. Turn your head away and you are in trouble. Cope with it or not, but everyone's scared.'

As a tourist he was magnificent. Just like a good wingman. When you thought you were the last man at the bar, he would pop up. Keeping his eye on you without seeming to. I reckon he thought he had a responsibility to make sure we didn't get ourselves into trouble when we were out on the squirts. Because he had such an amazing capacity to tolerate alcohol, he thought he should use his talent for good and not for evil.

Another thing that made him a great tourist was that you'd never know by his mood if he was making runs or not. The only measure of temperature with Boonie was how well the side was doing. If the side was doing well but he wasn't he'd still be as happy as anyone else. If he was making runs but the team wasn't winning, he'd be as pissed off as everyone. It was always about the team. Which is a great characteristic to have.

Boonie celebrated wins with more gusto than any other player. One time in South Africa, we'd won in Cape Town and we were staying in a hotel with reception on the left and lifts around to the right. We had a big, big night. Before we had gone out, the team manager had told us we were leaving at 10 the next morning, but our bags needed to be down in the foyer by 6 a.m. because our gear was being driven to the next destination and we were flying. Most players packed their bags and left them in the foyer before we hit the town, knowing that we weren't going to be in a particularly neat condition by the end of the night. Unfortunately, Boonie outsmarted himself.

He packed his bag and left it open in his room, leaving the clothes out that he was going to wear the next day. After our night out he gets back to the hotel, takes his clothes off, chucks them in the suitcase and locks it. Then he decides that he'll get a few extra hours sleep by taking his bag downstairs before he goes to bed. So he drags his case down to the foyer and, looking up, he sees the concierge running across the foyer to him. 'Mr Boon, I'll take your bag.'

'No, it's alright, I've got it.'

'Please let me take it, Mr Boon.'

'No it's okay, mate, I can do it.'

'But Mr Boon, you don't understand.'

'Don't understand what?'

'Mr Boon, you are naked!'

Ian Healy

Tests		
119 (1988–1999), 4356 runs (161 not out), 366 catches, 29 stumpings		
ODIs		
168 (1988–1997), 1764 runs, (56), 194 catches, 39 stumpings		

Ian Healy was a great cricketer. He is an even better bloke. He made his debut as a 23 year old and lasted eleven years. He brought some great qualities to the Australian side and one of the most important was an appreciation for other people's performances. I had been in and out of the Test team when he arrived and the side was rebuilding, but, for a young cricketer, it wasn't a great environment to be in. At that time, most players were worried about their own position in the side rather than how the side was doing. So if the side was beaten easily but a player performed well he was almost satisfied because he knew he was going to get the next game. The rest of us would be waiting around to get a tap on the shoulder.

Ian came in and showed a real understanding of the need to give young players confidence by getting them to concentrate on the positives. It didn't matter what the situation of the game was, whether the West Indies were two for 320—which they quite often were—or we were six for 35—which we quite often were—Ian always gave the impression that we were in control. He was upbeat, encouraging and supportive.

One thing I hadn't seen before was his reaction to a poor return from the outfield. We fast bowlers run in to bowl flat out and then between overs we are sent to cover acres of outfield while the batsmen, poor souls, have to stand still in the slips cordon and wave their arms around when they fail to stop the ball. So over the journey, exhausted as I was, I might have given a few less than perfect returns to the wicket-keeper. A lot of wicket-keepers, if there was a bad throw, would have their arms out and hands on their hips, their body language telling me I was a fool and a drag on the team. When Ian Healy got a bad return, he used to just pick it up and throw it to the bowler and wouldn't whinge or make a big deal about it. Heals just took it in his stride: I'm the wicket-keeper; I've got the gloves on. If you do a bad throw, it's up to me to make it look good.

As a bowler, the wicket-keeper is your best mate in the team. It's important to know how the ball is coming through and the wicket-keeper is the bloke that sees the best of you so he can tell you if you're falling away, and how you're getting through the crease. If Ian had a criticism of your bowling, he would always give you two or three positives first: 'Mate, mate you're hitting the crease really hard. You're getting through the crease. You're looking strong.

Your front arm is up nice and strong. Okay mate, you're going really well, but you can't bowl half volleys at three miles an hour. You reckon you can work on your pace?' He just said shit like that to get you going.

Most importantly, he understood how important the wicket-keeper is to the morale of the whole team. And a big part of that was having continuity with the wicket-keeper. We got used to having him there, and that meant he often had to endure great physical pain to keep playing. I hate to think how many matches he played with a broken thumb or finger. He was a great character and as tough as nails. He was a great teammate, Heals.

Mark Taylor

Tests
104 (1989–1999), 7525 runs (334 not out), 1 wicket (1 for 11), 157 catches

ODIs
113 (1989–1997), 3514 runs (105), 56 catches

Where do you start with Mark Taylor? Boring, left-handed opening batsman who, as a young bloke, wanted to captain Australia. No personality whatsoever. Right?

Mark Taylor is one of my all-time favourite teammates. He first got into the side under a cloud of controversy. Some thought that the selectors were in fact trying to pick Peter Taylor, or that Peter Taylor got in when they were trying to pick Mark Taylor. I don't know, it was all very confusing at the time. But Mark came in and immediately struck me as a level-headed, organised sort of bloke. He was a little bit serious but you can't expect too much more from an opening batsman!

He was lucky enough in his second Test match to be rooming with me. I always seemed to get blokes early in their careers. And if blokes who had been playing for a few years found they were rooming with me, they'd better start worrying: I think that was Bob Simpson and Allan Border's way of telling them they were on their last legs. If they didn't perform in that Test match they were out. My room was the last stop before the axing.

Mark's second Test match was at the Adelaide Oval. He'd made 25 and 3 in his debut, so he wasn't sure if he was coming or going when he was landed with me as a roomie. We were in the Hilton, on the fourteenth floor. We walked into the room and there it was: the little stretcher bed and the big double bed. Mark, with enthusiasm and genuine intent, said, 'Who gets the double bed?'

I said, 'How many Test teams have you made?'

'One.'

'Ha ha. Unlucky, Champ!' So he got the single stretcher bed.

The night before the game, the fire alarm goes off at 2 in the morning! Tubby turns all the lights on and sits on the edge of his bed. 'What's going on?' he asks.

In my most reassuring tone, I say, 'Mate, don't worry about it, it's probably a drill or a false alarm, go back to sleep.'

Of course, the serious opening batsman gets up, goes to the window and opens the curtain. 'Merv, come and have a look at this!'

I go to the window and there are fire trucks coming from everywhere! They park in front of the hotel, and a voice over the PA system booms, 'Guests in the Hotel

Hilton, this is not a drill. Please remain in your rooms until further notice.'

We're standing there watching these fire trucks coming and I lose interest pretty quickly and go and sit on my bed. Tubby doesn't move and I ask, 'What are you worried about?'

'I may never see my wife again.'

'Mark, ring her.'

'I can't ring her at 2 in the morning, she'll kill me!'

I say, 'Well you're going to die anyway so what difference does it make?'

I put my head back on the pillow and this alarm is still going and the lights are still on and Tubby is just sitting at the end of his bed and, despite my best efforts, he is still looking a bit nervous. I sit up and say, 'Mark, you're a smart man. Now, can you see smoke first or can you smell it?'

'I think you can smell it, Merv, I'm pretty sure you can smell it.'

'Alright then, can you turn the fuckin' lights off?'

That was his initiation into rooming with me. He went on in that Test match to earn the dubious distinction of being one of very few batsmen to be run out twice in one Test. Don't know if he was half asleep, but he certainly came up very short both times. And you can't blame me.

On the 1989 Ashes tour he made 839 runs. He could handle pace and late movement because he was so well organised at the crease. As a fieldsman, he was a sensation.

Fast bowlers battle all day to get an outside edge, and it was always good to see the ball heading towards Tubby. He was very good in the slips. Just organised, methodical. His talent at close-in catching was a huge bonus because he couldn't field anywhere that required too much running. So he fell on his feet there, didn't he?

He was a great leader. He vice-captained the side towards the end of my career and I knew that he was going to be a good captain. He had a different style to A.B. Tubs hated losing as much as anyone, but he always gave the impression of being unruffled, no matter what the game situation. A phlegmatic demeanour, but well organised and a quick thinker. He would be calm on the outside but you knew he was thinking hard underneath. When he was in charge, you knew he wouldn't take any shit, but he could let you know by making a sarcastic comment without going crook at you. He was always able to take the emotion out of any decision he made as a captain. That is a great quality to have in a leader. He learnt from A.B. the value of showing absolute loyalty to his players in public, but was very clear inside the sheds if you hadn't done what was expected.

When he took over the Australian captaincy from A.B., he did inherit a good side. He had some tough times with his own poor form when he took the reins. He couldn't get a run, and everyone was calling for his head. But there's not too many people who play Test cricket who don't go through tough times. They say tough times don't last, tough people do, and he became a very, very good captain. If you have a look at Mark Taylor and see that cuddly exterior you might think he's a bit soft. But mate, don't let that deceive you. He was one of the toughest blokes going around.

Justin Langer and Matthew Hayden

JUSTIN LANGER

Tests
105 (1993–2007), 7696 runs (250), 73 catches

ODIs
8 (1994–1997), 160 runs (36), 2 catches, 1 stumping

MATTHEW HAYDEN

Tests
103 (1994–2009), 8625 runs (380), 128 catches

ODIs
161 (1993–2008), 6133 runs (181 not out), 68 catches

T20Is
9 (2005–2007), 308 runs (73 not out), 1 catch

Matthew Hayden and Justin Langer were Australia's most successful opening combination and one of the best in the history of cricket. They remind me of the movie *Twins*—Danny DeVito and Arnold Schwarzenegger (although I think Justin may have been a little bit fitter and stronger than Danny DeVito). They formed a great partnership for a long time, but they both struggled hard before they found themselves together at the top of the order.

Justin made a name for himself as a gritty, determined player but he turned into a free-flowing opener. He made his debut in 1993 against the West Indies in Adelaide. He was batting at number three on a pitch that wasn't helpful for batsmen. We rolled the mighty West Indian line-up for 146 in the second innings, leaving us with 186 to win. He played a really tough, grafting innings, and made 54. The only other top-order batsman to make double figures was Mark Waugh, with 26. He was the ninth man out, having batted with Tim May to get to about 40 short of the target. In his first Test! I thought after that innings: He's going to be the next Allan Border. He's going to be the mainstay of an innings. He's going to hold down that middle order and be someone that Australia can build the next generation around. Four Tests later he made two ducks against New Zealand and then didn't make the 1993 Ashes touring squad. Cricket really does test a player's character.

He got back into the Australian team for the Third Test on the tour of Pakistan in November 1994, batting at number seven. He made 69 in the only innings of the drawn game. His next Test was in December 1996. He then played a string of Tests, mainly at number three, but by the time of the 2001 Ashes tour, he was out of favour. He toured but it wasn't until the Fifth Test that he played, and he replaced Michael Slater, opening with Matthew Hayden. With 102 not out, Justin had finally found his spot, eight years after his debut.

The thing that always struck me about J.L. was his courage. The tougher it got, and the more conflict in the game, the more he stood up. At the MCG in 2004/05 against Pakistan, Shoaib Akhtar was bowling at the speed of light and Justin was wearing it and looking very uncomfortable. He got through it and made 50, and when he came off, said that it was the most excited he'd ever been playing Test cricket. He just loved it. Insane.

The thing that intrigued me was the size of him. You wouldn't think he's a threat, but he is a black belt in about ten different martial arts and he is not afraid to show it when you give him a little bit of lip.

I found out about that on our first tour together to New Zealand in 1993. We were giving him a bit of a hard time, and he got these crazy eyes and got the karate chops out. Big bully me taunted him with, 'What are you going to do? Get your little black belt on me?' I reckon within a split second his foot was about 2 inches away from my face. Didn't say a word. Just smiled at me and walked away. That shut me up!

Matthew Hayden is just the opposite. A mountain of a man. He intimidated through sheer size. I played against him a lot, and even when he let the ball go, he would bring the bat up over his head, show me the full face of it from the top and look down the wicket at me. It made me wonder,

Who is supposed to be intimidating who here? He is just a big bloke. I used to call him 'Unit' because that's what he is: one big unit.

Some people think Haydos was a slogger, but he was never a slogger. He was just a very technically correct hard hitter of the ball and wasn't afraid to go over the top.

On the 1993 Ashes tour, he had just got into the squad—a kid from the country, just loving life. An Ashes tour can be pretty demanding, especially for a young bloke getting used to living out of a suitcase for four months in England. So us senior players would get put with the young blokes early on to help them out. Well I don't know if I helped him out at all but we had one of the best shaving-cream fights of all time. At one point I split my eye on the doorway as I was trying to get away from him, so he claimed victory. Mate, he had more shaving cream on him than I did!

Unit took a long time to get into the Test team. He made his first-class debut in 1991. He went to England in 1993, where he opened in the one dayers, and he and Michael Slater were the options for opening with Mark Taylor in the Tests. Slats and Haydos were pretty even chances for the spot but the reasoning came down to not wanting two left-handed opening batsmen, so Slats got in and did really well. But Unit didn't drop his bundle on the tour—he made 1150 first-class runs. No one had scored 1000 first-class runs on an Ashes tour without playing Test matches. That showed the depth that he had and we knew that once Matthew got an opportunity he was going to be okay.

I've coupled Matthew Hayden and Justin Langer together, since together they were a formidable opening partnership for Australia for a long time and quite often led the way for the Australians in tough run chases in second innings. They made a very difficult thing look easy for a long time. But individually, too, they were both fine cricketers and are fine men. Justin made more than 28,000 first-class runs and 23 Test centuries. Haydos made 30 Test centuries and finished his career with a Test average better than 50. As an opener, facing the new ball every time he batted, that is a phenomenal performance. Obviously I helped him get where he did, with those early lessons about coping with the grind of a tour. I only got to room with him that one time, though. I couldn't afford to room with him anymore. Ran out of shaving cream.

Mark Waugh

Tests
128 (1991–2002), 8029 runs (153 not out), 59 wickets (5 for 40), 181 catches

ODIs
244 (1988–2002), 8500 runs (173), 85 wickets (5 for 24), 108 catches

I made my One Day International debut in the same match as Mark Waugh, against Pakistan at Adelaide in 1988. Who do you reckon won Man of the Match? That's right, me. It didn't help him much that we bowled first on a wet wicket and got them out for 177, then he didn't get a bat. Even so, at that stage of our careers, I was a better one-day player than he was. Mark went on to be one of the greatest one-day all-rounders of his time. He was inventive with the bat, useful with the ball and magical in the field. As a close-in fieldsman he was second to none, but he could also throw down the stumps from the boundary. Behind Jamie Siddons, Mark Waugh was the second-best fieldsman I ever played with.

You expect twins to be alike in so many ways, and Steve and Mark were very different in so many more. Unlike Steve, Mark was pretty quiet. But it was evident from his contributions to team meetings that he had a great cricket brain. One of his greatest insights into the game was during the Test series in the West Indies in 1991. He was copping an absolute battering, and by the time we got to the Fifth Test he came to the conclusion that if you're batting defensively you're waiting to get out so you might as well score runs. This was only his seventh Test, and he was facing Patrick Patterson, Curtly Ambrose, Courtney Walsh and Malcolm Marshall. Four bowlers who were lethal with the ball. The West Indies were just going at him hard and he was playing shots over slips and playing pulls and hooks, and he looked like he was going to get out every ball. He made 139 not out and set up the win. That was his mindset. Because he was such a very, very talented cricketer, he had the ability to do things in his own way.

He looked very casual and blasé at the crease and before I really got to know him, at times he looked as though he didn't care and that frustrated me. But once I had got to know him, I knew that his relaxed approach was how he countered nerves.

Mark Waugh was an incredible talent with a quite remarkable mind about the game of cricket.

Keith Miller

Tests

55 (1946–1956), 2958 runs (147), 170 wickets (7 for 60), 38 catches

When your life is playing cricket, you spend a lot of time with cricketers, talking cricket. And it's not always taking the piss out of teammates. Players in any team talk about famous victories and the players involved. Sometimes, you hear about legendary cricketers, but not necessarily for their play . . .

Keith Miller was one of Tony Dodemaide's favourite players and when Dodders and I played for Victoria, Dodders used to talk about him all the time—Keith Miller this, Keith Miller that. At that stage I didn't have any idea of his stature so I just nodded and agreed. Although he was considered an all-rounder, he batted at number four or five and usually opened the bowling, so could have held his spot in the team for either. Apparently a good-looking critter in his day, he cut a fair swathe through the dance floor too.

But the reason Keith Miller intrigued me was because of one quote. Talking about pressure in Test cricket, Miller, who was a fighter pilot in the Second World War, apparently said, 'Listen boys, you don't know what pressure is until you've got a Messerschmitt up your arse at 3200 feet.'

Here's this bloke who's been through it all, played football for St Kilda and Victoria, flew planes in the war, and treated Test cricket as a game to be enjoyed. Puts things in perspective, doesn't it?

Warwick Armstrong

Tests

50 (1902–1921), 2863 runs (159 not out), 87 wickets (6 for 35), 44 catches

Another cricketer from the past that seemed to get mentioned a lot in the Australian changing rooms was Warwick 'The Big Ship' Armstrong. Quite often in sport people get ridiculed about their size—given a hard time because they are oversize—and I have never understood it. The Big Ship was certainly oversize. Someone reckoned he got to 21 stone by his last Test. Apparently the only things he liked more than a feed were a fight and a glass of whiskey. The talk of how big, how powerful and how bold a person he was always interested me. And any bloke as keen on the fang as the Big Ship must have been, was always going to be someone I looked up to.

He was one of Australia's best all-rounders, and one of the few players to captain Australia to a 5–nil defeat of the Poms in an Ashes series. The only other blokes to do it were Ricky Ponting in 2006/07, and Michael Clarke in 2013/14. He was 42 when he played his last Test, and made more than 16,000 first-class runs. Obviously, being overweight didn't affect *his* longevity. He also didn't mind taking on authority and it sounds like he didn't mind the world knowing he was a smartarse. He disliked draws and thought that Tests should be played until a result was decided. This was at a time when Tests were scheduled for only three days' play. In the Fourth Test of the 1921 Ashes tour, the first day, a Saturday, saw no play because of rain. Sunday being Sunday was a rest day. At ten to six on the Monday afternoon, Armstrong finished bowling an over and England declared at 4 for plenty, giving Australia half an hour to bat before the close. The batsmen departed, but Armstrong refused to leave the field, and sat on the pitch. Eventually, he reminded the umpires that there had been a rule amendment in 1914 that stated that if the first day had been lost to rain, a declaration could not be made within an hour and 40 minutes of the end of play. The umpires conceded, the English batsmen were recalled, and Armstrong bowled the next over, just to show he could get away with two in a row!

His skill and the force of his personality made him one of Australia's most successful captains, and some say he was our version of W.G. Grace and the father of modern cricket. We're still waiting for the DNA results to get back from the lab on that one, but the dressing room talk about what a huge man he was built him up in my mind to be something of a Colossus. Then one day at the MCG cricket museum I saw one of the shirts that he wore. I was really disappointed. I looked at his shirt and thought, 'He wasn't that big, he was just an Extra Large.'

Stan McCabe

Tests

39 (1930–1938), 2748 runs (232), 36 wickets (4 for 13), 41 catches

I had never heard Stan McCabe's name before 1993. We were talking about great Ashes victories while we were touring around England, when the bus driver said, 'Does anyone want to see Stonehenge? It's up on the left and you might be able to see it through the left side windows.'

Cultured cricketers that we were, the reaction he got was, 'What's Ston'enge?'

Paul Reiffel said, 'That's the bundle of rocks Chevy Chase backed into in *European Vacation*,' so of course then everyone knew what it was and we all crowded on that side of the bus to see it.

At that point Steve Waugh starts banging on again about the great Australian cricket traditions and throwing some names around. Brendon Julian has no idea.

'Neil Harvey?' says Brendon, 'Who's he? What did he do?'

'You probably don't even know who Stan McCabe is, do you?' says Steve.

B.J. says, in all seriousness, 'Was he in *Jake and the Fatman*?'

So Stan McCabe from that day became a legend—not because he was a great cricketer but because we all thought he was in *Jake and the Fatman*.

Brendon Julian

Tests
7 (1993–1995), 128 runs (56 not out), 15 wickets (4 for 36), 4 catches

ODIs
25 (1993–1999), 224 runs (35), 22 wickets (3 for 40), 8 catches

Brendon Julian is the perfect example of how statistics in cricket don't necessarily tell the story of the capabilities or the impact of a player.

He was such a smooth bowler with such a simple action, his bowling style was effortless—if occasionally wayward. If you didn't know him you would think he wasn't trying or he didn't care. But that was just him. Although he looked casual, within the team, we knew that he was a very talented, skilful cricketer and that he really wanted to be successful. Unfortunately for B.J., his Test career started at the same time as one Glenn McGrath, so it was hard to get a spot. But he had enormous potential and on his day he was an absolute superstar.

B.J. was on the Ashes tour in 1993, and made his Test debut in the First Test at the Old Trafford ground in Manchester. He bowled well, and took three wickets. The plan for the bowling attack in the Second Test was Shane Warne and Tim May as the two spinners, Craig McDermott and I to bowl fast, with the Waugh brothers and Allan Border to pitch in if we needed. So B.J. got dropped after his first Test. Then McDermott got injured in the Second Test, so Brendon came back into the side for the Third Test at Trent Bridge.

By the Third Test, we were 2–nil up in the series and we led on the first innings, but England knew the series was on the line and Thorpe and Gooch both got centuries in the second innings. We lost a couple of wickets and we came in at tea on the last day six wickets down, needing more than 200 to win—an unrealistic target without wickets in hand. B.J. and Steve Waugh were batting and we only had Warne, May and me to come. So at tea Allan Border talked to the five of us who had to save the match about the importance of holding up an end and not playing any loose shots. Actually, he talked to the four of us— Brendon was on the dunny so he hadn't heard the rev up from A.B.

As he's putting the pads on to go back on the ground, he says, 'A.B., we going for these runs or not?' A.B. just looks at him and shakes his head and then walks out of the room, saying, 'Is he for real?' So we all have a laugh at the young buck taking the piss out of A.B.

First over after tea, B.J. smashes one down the ground for four. A.B. just holds his head in his hands and says, 'So we are going for these runs!'

B.J. made 56 not out. For a bloke who is seen as so laid-back and so relaxed, to see him bat with such surety and confidence, under the pump and in his second Test match, was a testament to the sort of bloke he is. He batted the entire final session, outscored Steve Waugh and saved an Ashes Test.

B.J.'s crowning glory was the 1995 tour of the West Indies, alongside Paul Reiffel. Playing the best Test team in the world, a team that had been at the top for twenty years, B.J. took four of the first six wickets on the first day of the First Test, and that set the tone for the series.

The other side of B.J.'s value to the team was the fact he was a sensational tourist. He has that knack of saying funny things without trying to be funny. On a tour you could just look at him and start laughing because you knew he would be about to say something silly. And hasn't he done well? Looks good, played a bit of cricket, camera loves him: get *him* on the telly and don't worry about us fat ugly blokes!

Bob Simpson

Tests

62 (1957–1978), 4869 runs (311), 71 wickets (5 for 57), 110 catches

My first Test match was during Bob Simpson's first series as coach of the Australian side. He and I came together at a turning point for cricket in Australia.

Bob had retired from Test cricket in 1968, then been recalled as captain during the World Series Cricket turmoil. Then in 1985/86, he was appointed as Australia's first coach.

During my first training session with the Australian side, I had finished bowling and was having a spell and a drink. Bob came to me and said, 'Get your pads on.'

I don't think I had batted at state training for more than eighteen months. 'I think I'll be right without a bat,' I told him.

'Well put your pads on and run laps for twenty minutes.'

'Okay, I'll have a bat.'

Bob was determined for every bowler to be able to make runs, for every batsman to be able to bowl if things got tight, and for everyone to be able to influence a game through their fielding. Everyone.

He taught me that I had to always consider my responsibilities to the team. Off the field, it was about being well prepared, well presented and respectful of the privilege of representing my country. On the field, it was about always being aware of the momentum of the game and doing what was best for the team in any circumstance. If I was batting with a batsman, I had to make sure I was never dismissed by playing a risky shot. If I was batting with a bowler, it was: swing hard and swing often, because we weren't there for long. That's why he had such a huge impact on me. Probably because he knew he had to give me simple goals and simple instructions! He was one of the most important influences on the player I became.

His influence over the team, when we were really struggling as a unit, was enormous. He made it clear what was expected, and left the rest to the individual to respond or to be dropped. He had the respect of the players because of his record as a player and a captain, and he respected us. He had high but straightforward expectations about our skills and our fitness and he laid the foundations for Australia to become the best Test and One Day team in the world. He changed Australian cricket forever.

Paul Reiffel

Tests

35 (1992–1998), 955 runs (79 not out), 104 wickets (6 for 71), 15 catches

ODIs

92 (1992–1999), 503 runs (58), 106 wickets (4 for 13), 25 catches

As laid-back as Brendon Julian was, Paul Reiffel was ten times more laid-back and more casual. Even when he ran Pistol looked like he was jogging.

He was a very underrated bowler for many years, especially by Victoria and the Victorian hierarchy, but Bob Simpson and the selectors saw something in him and he really developed when he got into the Australian side. That says something about the man: to improve by playing at the highest level shows how committed he was to getting the best out of himself.

I don't think I've seen a better bowler to left-handed batsmen. Pistol had patience. He bowled in close to the stumps, bowled it middle and off and just nibbled away. He could get the ball to deviate off the seam in both directions, and because he was so upright and so straight, he didn't need much deviation to get an edge.

His performance in the 1993 Ashes tour was outstanding. Pistol had been a bit surprised to be selected for the tour, as he hadn't played for Australia against the West Indies the preceding summer at home, and had only taken five wickets in three Tests in New Zealand. He bowled very well in some tour games but had to wait until the Fourth Test to make an appearance. Craig McDermott had returned to Australia with colic, and with the match to be played at Headingley, somewhere that always had something for enterprising quick bowlers, the plan had been to play the three seamers: Pistol, Brendon Julian and me. Unfortunately B.J. was injured, but it meant Pistol got to open the bowling in his first Ashes Test and only his fifth Test match. He took five for 65 in the first innings. That showed the strength of Pistol's character and his absolute commitment to the game. Then he buttered up with six for 71 in the first innings of the Fifth Test. He took nineteen wickets in three Tests.

The peak of his Test career was in the West Indies in 1995. McDermott was injured again, Brendon Julian's previous Test match for Australia was his second (on the Ashes tour in 1993), and Glenn McGrath had only played nine Tests. So Pistol was leading a hopelessly inexperienced attack against the Test team that had been the best in the world for twenty years and hadn't lost a home series to Australia since 1973. In the final and deciding Fourth Test, Pistol was the best of the bowlers in the first innings, taking three for 48. Australia then made 531 with a Steve Waugh double century. On the final session of the penultimate day,

Pistol took the first three wickets, including Brian Lara, lbw for a duck, setting up the victory.

In the field Pistol was very, very safe. With the bat, he was organised and dependable, reliable—whatever word you want to use—and a great teammate. He didn't say much but what he said was worth listening to.

Later in his career, he was held in really high esteem by everyone that played cricket with him, and by many who played against him. That respect people have for him has helped his new career as an ICC Elite Panel International Umpire.

He was also highly respected by his teammates off the field. We dubbed him 'The Wingman' in both the Victorian and the Australian sides. We'd all be out having a few beers. Sometime in the night I'd look around and there would be no one else there. I'd look at my watch and think, This is a bit weak, it's only 2 a.m., and we haven't got a game tomorrow. This is ridiculous! I'd start to think it was time to go home. Then I'd glance over my shoulder and there Paul would be with his Southern and Coke; just raise his glass, give a little smile and that reassuring look that said, I'm here, I'm not going anywhere. I'm with ya. That's what he was like on the ground too. We could always depend on him to do a job for the team.

Tony Dodemaide

Tests
10 (1987–1992), 202 runs (50), 34 wickets (6 for 58), 6 catches

ODIs
24 (1988–1993), 124 runs (30), 36 wickets (5 for 21), 7 catches

First Class
184 (1983–1998), 5966 runs (123), 534 wickets (6 for 58), 89 catches

Tony Dodemaide: 'The Great Man' as he was and still is known at the Footscray Cricket Club. The second-nicest bloke you will ever meet and anyone that has met his brother Alan will confirm that.

Doddy got to Footscray a couple of years after me and was a very talented young player. Ron Gaunt must have asked him to bat when he first arrived, because they let Dodders be an all-rounder! I became very, very good mates with him, although he reminds me that when he first got down to Footscray playing in the 2nds and 3rds I didn't talk to him. I don't think that's right but he brings it up after a few beers every now and then.

Dodders was a great cricketer and a great teammate.

You never had qualms about him ever shirking an issue, or ever giving less than he had. He played a lot of games for Victoria, played a lot of games for Footscray. Played Test matches, and was the first player in cricket to take five wickets in his One Day International debut. He made 50 in his first Test innings, against a New Zealand team with Richard Hadlee at the top of his form. Dodders then took six wickets in the second innings. Nice opening effort! He also played a lot of county cricket at Sussex to hone his skills, and became very, very good in English conditions. It didn't matter what level he played, he just gave his all. And his all was very good.

He wasn't the type of bowler who would regularly rip through an opposition, but the more overs he bowled, the more likely he was to take a wicket. He had a very simple approach to bowling, particularly on third and fourth day wickets: just run in, hit the seam and allow for natural variation. His biggest assets were his efficiency and his accuracy. He could bowl lumps of overs, putting the ball on the same spot every time and building pressure on a batsman.

In Wangaratta in a Shield game, one of our opening batsmen was injured and Queensland had made a heap of runs, bowled us out for less than the follow on and put us back in. Dodders was 71 not out, and in the second innings opened the batting. He made 47 in an opening partnership of 110 with Dav Whatmore against the might of Craig McDermott, and helped save the game. So he could bat anywhere—probably six or seven pulled him up most of the time but if asked to bat up the order he did anything that the team wanted or needed him to do.

He is CEO of Cricket Victoria now and doing a great job there. He had the same position at the Western Australia Cricket Association, and was the MCC's Head of Cricket at Lord's. He gets those types of jobs because he is one of the best-organised blokes I know.

He has given me advice on several occasions. He's stirred me up a few times; he does tend to give me a rocket when I need it. He's one of those blokes: you don't take offence to what he says because he's always trying to do what is good for you. A couple of times I've tapped into his mind to get myself right. Years ago, in 1988/89, I had taken one for 182 in the first two Shield matches of the season and things weren't going that well. I couldn't get a wicket, couldn't buy a wicket, was being slogged everywhere.

I was at club training one night, and I thought, I really don't want to bowl tonight. I'll go for a run. After about 5 kilometres I stopped and thought, What the hell am I doing? I walked back to the ground, got in the rooms, sat down. I was sitting there, gutted. Dod's walked in the room and said, 'What's wrong with you?'

'Just trying to figure out whether I want to keep playing or not.'

'Right. Jump in the car.' We ended up at his place. Got a slab. Had a talk about life in general. Dodders was great at deep insight. Knew the big questions and when to ask them.

'Where do you work, Merv?' he asked.

'At a warehouse in South Melbourne.'

'Are you going to work there for the rest of your life?'

'Well, it seems like a good option.'

'Pull your head out of your arse, big fella. Have a think about life.'

I took ten wickets in the next Shield match, and made the 1989 Ashes tour. Happy days.

Jason Gillespie

Tests
71 (1996–2006), 1218 runs (201 not out), 259 wickets (7 for 37), 27 catches

ODIs
97 (1996–2005), 289 runs (44 not out), 142 wickets (5 for 22), 10 catches

Dizzy Gillespie was one of the most awesome bowlers I have ever seen play. I have no qualms in naming him one of my favourite cricketers. When he bowled he was tenacious and unrelenting, and at his peak he was a powerful, dangerous bowler. In partnership with Glenn McGrath, occasionally Brett Lee or Michael Kasprowicz, he was outstanding. His run-up, his action—he just threw himself down the wicket and the pace that he generated was thrilling to watch.

Compared with that, his batting was a little disappointing (although he did get a double century not out against Bangladesh . . .). On the other hand, his batting was where his sense of humour came out. When he and Glenn McGrath were making some runs against New Zealand in 2004 at the Gabba and he got his 50, he put the bat between his legs and galloped around like he was on a broomstick pony. A lot of people saw that as him being cocky and arrogant, and demeaning to New Zealand. But he doesn't have an arrogant bone in his body. Those who knew him knew that he was just having a good laugh, not taking himself too seriously. He would never have thought it would cause offence, because he was just recognising that he had made a milestone in a game he loved. There was clearly something wrong with the pitch that day because McGrath made 61, Dizzy got 54 not out and Australia made 585. New Zealand were all out in the second innings for 76 . . .

Dizzy missed almost as many Tests through injury as he played. The effort he put into his bowling took its toll. So did trying to take a catch in Sri Lanka in the First Test of the 1999 series. Dizzy was running in from the boundary, Steve Waugh was running from the in-field with the flight of the ball. They both left the ground in an air ambulance.

At state level I played against him in 1998/99 when I was playing for the mighty Canberra Comets, the side that represented the Australian Capital Territory for three seasons in the domestic one-day competition. Jason was bowling at one end and they had a spinner at the other. I was number ten, batting with Lea Hansen. When I got to the wicket I said to Lea, 'We'll just push singles, we have time, and we need to just accumulate whatever we can.'

Lea replied, 'I'm not pushing any singles. I'm not facing Gillespie, he's bowling too quick.'

To which I replied, 'Mate, I'm 37 and finished, you just get down there and take your medicine, Champ.'

Dizzy ran in and bowled the first ball, and I nicked it. He had two slips and it went wide of them, too fine for third man, and I got a four. The next ball, he bowled a bouncer. I got back to hook it and by the time I thought about bringing my bat around, the ball had hit the keeper's gloves. I asked Jamie Siddons that night why he had bounced me. Jamie reckoned he was trying to scare me. I said to Jamie, 'Tell him it was too late. I was already shitting myself when I walked out to bat!'

Dizzy Gillespie is an outstanding bloke off the ground, but when he was bowling he was nasty. He would do what he could to scare you, and then he'd get you out. You've just got to love a bloke like that, haven't you?

Allan Border

Tests
156 (1979–1994), 11,174 runs (205), 39 wickets (7 for 46), 156 catches

ODIs
273 (1979–1994), 6524 runs (127 not out), 73 wickets (3 for 20), 127 catches

Allan Border was my captain in all of my 53 Tests. I got into the Australian team when we had lost players to the rebel tour to South Africa. A.B. had only captained the side for twelve matches, our performances had been poor for a couple of years, and we had a very young side. His first Test match as captain was in December 1984, and my first Test was in December 1985. There were only two blokes who played in both matches: A.B. and David Boon. Geoff Marsh and Bruce Reid made their debut with me and three of my teammates, Wayne Phillips, David Hookes and Ray Bright never played Test cricket with me again. That shows how rapidly Australian cricket was changing and the amount of pressure A.B. was under as a new captain.

His fundamental leadership philosophy was unqualified public support for all of his players. When there was any public criticism of the team he'd go to the media and stick up for the players, often when he had no right to. Great captain. Great communicator. He led by example. He didn't really make a big deal or a fuss of things on the ground, and he copped a lot of criticism about that. But within the environment of the change rooms he would explain your role within the team and let you know what he expected from you. If you didn't do the job he would let you know about that, too. He wouldn't ask the players to do anything he wouldn't do himself so if we were hammered at training for a bad performance he would suffer with the rest of us. Not the quickest, the strongest, the most physically talented bloke but the harder the training got, the hotter it was, the taller he stood.

His first four years as skipper were really tough going for him, there is no doubt about that, with the young side and lack of results. Then Australia went to the World Cup on the subcontinent in 1987 as underdogs and came back as winners. That had a big impact on the level of confidence inside the team. The atmosphere that A.B. and Bob Simpson had created was one where the players were starting to realise what could be achieved. Next Australia beat New Zealand in a series in Australia, and lost 1–nil in Pakistan. Then in 1988/89, we got flogged by the West Indies in Australia.

The team that was selected for the 1989 Ashes tour was still a work in progress. We were heading to England hoping to regain the Ashes, something that had not been done in England for 50 years, and the English media were describing us as the worst team to have ever left Australia's shores.

What a lot of people don't realise is that Allan Border played county cricket for two years, in 1986 and 1988, for Essex, Graham Gooch's county. During that time, he had honed his game for English conditions, and got to know the enemy very well. He had developed bowling plans for every player he came across. During the 1989 Ashes, players new to the English team, like Tim Curtis and Kim Barnett, were familiar to A.B. and he had a plan for each of them.

He had watched Graham Gooch more than anyone, and he developed a strategy to get him. A.B. set what was then a pretty radical field, with two short mid-wickets. He knew that Gooch made most of his runs through the leg side. He would take the ball off the stumps, even outside the off stump, and swing it through the leg side. A.B. knew Gooch occasionally played the ball uppishly, so he placed the field accordingly and occasionally, instead of trying to tie Gooch down by bowling outside off, we would feed him on the leg side. The two men at short mid-wicket meant Gooch had to change his game.

Allan Border used the 1989 Ashes tour to set a new standard for Australian cricket teams. As well as his meticulous planning, he made some tough leadership decisions. Wives and girlfriends were not to stay with players at the team hotel because he didn't want the players to think they were in England for a holiday. We were there to do a job.

He also brought the mongrel back into the Australian side. He had noticed that the English treated cricket like a game, and he decided that wasn't the way that Australians should play Test cricket. A lot of players have great skill, and he knew that if they were not pressured, if their temperament was not tested, they could score freely. A.B. decided we weren't going to let that happen. (Still to this day, when the Australians are playing as a team and getting in the face of the opposition, they can put the skill and temperament of whichever team they're playing under immense pressure.) He just enforced that we were there to win, and we were to train hard and play hard. That was all he expected. We won the First Test by 210 runs and the series 4–nil.

The mongrel was back, and A.B. had shown what preparation, planning and confidence could do for a team. The 1989 Ashes tour was a turning point for Australian cricket and a turning point for me as a cricketer. It was due to the remarkable leadership of Allan Border.

Ray Bright

Tests
25 (1977–1986), 445 runs (33), 53 wickets (7 for 87), 13 catches

ODIs
11 (1974–1986), 66 runs (19 not out), 3 wickets (1 for 28), 2 catches

Ray Bright played in the most interesting of times for Test cricket in Australia. He saw the turmoil of World Series cricket and although he didn't play a lot of Test matches, he was a critical part of the rebuilding of Australian cricket because of his experience and his ability to inspire his teammates to work to improve their games.

I played club cricket with him at Footscray as a young bloke. He used to come back and play when he wasn't representing Australia and Victoria and I always held him in high regard. He was originally from Spotswood, hence his nickname Spotty. His other nickname was Casper, because they reckoned his bowling was like Casper the Friendly Ghost: there was no fear to it. But that was a bit harsh. Ray played in the not-so-famous tied Test, against India in Madras in 1986. He and Greg Matthews each took five wickets in the second innings, to dismiss India for 347 and tie the match.

We didn't see a hell of a lot of Ray at Footscray when he had national and state duties but when he did turn up, he brought another dimension to batting and bowling in the nets. Everyone felt the pressure to train at a higher intensity when he was around. His whole approach was about quality. What Ray brought to training was an enormously competitive edge to everything we did. Virtually every ball he bowled, he made a contest of it. For a young bloke, that was a real eye opener.

When I got into the state side, he was one of the senior players there. He was also one of the senior blokes in the Australian side in 1985 in my first Test match in Adelaide. It was comforting to have him there. The step into Test match cricket is the biggest leap a player makes, and you need senior players there to show you the way. That's why it's so hard to build a team if you haven't got a number of hardened Test cricket team leaders. Blokes like Ray Bright probably didn't get the recognition they deserved, because he was one of the blokes we all depended on when we were learning how to be Test cricketers.

But some of my best memories of him were from our Sheffield Shield days. Crowds at Sheffield Shield matches are not large but are particularly loyal. The same fans seem to be at most of the matches. Spotty particularly liked one bloke who used to come to our matches at the MCG. His line, which we used to hang out for on the last day of every

Shield match, was, 'Ay Spotty, give him the one that spins!' There were always ten players who enjoyed it, although Ray didn't seem to see the funny side of it.

Darren Lehmann

Tests
27 (1998–2004), 1798 runs (177), 15 wickets (3 for 42), 11 catches

ODIs
117 (1996–2005), 3078 runs (119), 52 wickets (4 for 7), 26 catches

First Class
284 (1987–2007), 25,795 runs (339), 130 wickets (4 for 35), 143 catches

Darren got into the South Australia side as a twelve year old, from memory, and was a little, rotund, left-handed batsman and we hated him. Then he came to Victoria and we loved him because we didn't have to bowl to him.

There was an innings in Adelaide in 1989/90 when South Australia was struggling a bit and Victoria had a pretty good attack. O'Donnell, Dodemaide, Reiffel and me—young Darren Lehmann made us look like school kids. We couldn't beat him for pace and he would smile quietly to himself as he hit the ball wherever he wanted. I would bowl on off stump and he would push me through cover. So then I would take a bloke from the leg side and move him to cover to stop that shot and then bowl him exactly the same ball. Instead of taunting me a little by playing a shot just wide of where I had put the new fieldsman, he would swing the ball through the gap I had created on the leg side! Then I would take a slip out to plug up that hole, bowl in the same spot, and he would play a late cut through the just-vacated slip. He just enjoyed taking the piss out of the bowler. Watching him play, it wasn't hard to tell he had been captained in his early years by David Hookes.

He was an amazingly good batsman. He made more than 25,000 runs in first-class cricket, at an average of 57.8. That is an amazing batting record. He came to Victoria and continued to pile on the runs, and questions began to be asked about why he wasn't in the Test team. At the time the Test line-up was Geoff Marsh, Mark Taylor, David Boon, Allan Border, Dean Jones and Steve Waugh—so who are you going to drop? He should have played more Test matches but unfortunately selectors can only pick eleven. Someone has to miss out. The test of a good side is not the players in the team, it's the players who can't get a game.

As a player, Darren was highly competitive but he was very carefree with the way he played his game, just like his South Australian skipper. He loves winning and celebrates with the best of them, but underneath it isn't the be-all-and-end-all for him. His philosophy is: If we win, we win. If we lose, there is always tomorrow. At the same time, he is uncompromising in his preparation, and you know that as a coach he would be going out of his way to prepare the team to be the best they could possibly be.

Lehmann is one of the very few coaches who understand that a team can't win every match. There are going to be players who have bad days, there are going to be opposition that have exceptionally good days. The toss of the coin, the conditions and the weather are variables that can't be controlled. He is very thoughtful and very methodical. He would have a strong desire to win every game, but the impression he gives is that as long as the players are at their best, we can cop that.

As a coach, Darren takes a genuine interest in each player's life outside cricket because he believes that if everything is balanced, you're going to play better cricket. So he wants the blokes to involve their families, to involve their friends and to feel comfortable. He goes that extra step to make sure that everyone is happy and content. At the same time, if the players step out of line, he will be ruthless in letting them know they are letting down the team. He expects players to be entirely committed to being the best they can be. His approach is a bit of a contrast to A.B.'s, but a captain needs to have a harder edge because he is leading the team into battle. A coach's job is to make sure the team is as well prepared as possible.

This idea that it is only a game is not softness. I think that is one of the great things about cricket. It is a test of your character to be as aggressive and competitive as possible on the field, to do anything and everything within the rules to win, and then be able to step off the field and have a beer with your opponent at the end of play. It's easy to take a grudge into the showers—it's much tougher to leave it on the ground.

Glenn McGrath

Tests
124 (1993–2007), 641 runs (61), 563 wickets (8 for 24), 38 catches

ODIs
250 (1993–2007), 115 runs (11), 381 wickets (7 for 15), 37 catches

T20Is
2 (2005), 5 runs (5), 5 wickets (3 for 31), 1 catch

Glenn's biggest strength was his biggest weakness. His consistency. You knew where he was going to bowl: back of a length, off stump. I loved the way he worked batsmen out. He would start bowling in the corridor 9 inches outside off stump, and if the batsman was playing at him he kept it there. If the batsman wasn't playing at him he would get a little bit closer to off stump. He worked across that corridor until the batsman started to play at him and then he just hung around there.

His longevity in the game is a credit to him. He didn't overextend himself—and didn't have to, being 6 foot 5 in the old scale—bowling at no quicker than 140 kilometres per hour (although in his younger days he was a bit quicker).

If anyone was game enough to take him on he didn't really have a change of pace. He didn't change his length that much either. He occasionally bowled a bouncer, or bowled a good yorker, but that back of a length ball from 6 foot 5 that hit the splice of the bat was a very effective weapon. He had a very efficient action that didn't wear him down but it would slowly increase the pressure until the batsman was ground into the dirt.

He was extraordinary. He got the ball in the right place to left-handers or right-handers, both over the wicket and around the wicket, and was just so consistent. Being as tall as he was, he had the power to get bounce off the wicket rather than pace through the wicket. And at the top level it is bounce that is the more powerful weapon.

But Glenn was as dangerous as anyone when he bowled short. He tried to get the blokes hooking by getting it over a shoulder, or he tried to get into their rib cage to make it uncomfortable for batting, and because of his height, he could do that without bowling as short as other bowlers needed to.

Of course, I take most of the credit for his success, because Glenn took my spot in the Test team and his rise and my fall were so quick that I didn't have a chance to take him under my wing! I didn't have a lot to do with him apart from touring with him in South Africa in 1994. I was worried about my spot and we had Paul Reiffel and Damien Fleming with us so with two young Victorians in the squad you're not really going to waste your time on a

New South Welshman, are you? So helping a young Glenn McGrath wasn't high on my agenda—and didn't that work out well for him!

I think he could have kept playing and it was really disappointing when he decided to retire. When I got on the selection panel I was looking forward to one thing more than anything: He replaced me in the Australian side, so it's going to be great when it comes time to drop him. But I never got my satisfaction as he retired before I could do that!

Wayne B. Phillips

Tests
27 (1983–1986), 1485 runs (159), 52 catches

ODIs
48 (1982–1986), 852 runs (75 not out), 42 catches

Two blokes with the same name, and I played a single Test match with each of them. You should be able to win a free drink with that fact.

Wayne Phillips 1 was a wicket-keeper/batsman from South Australia who launched the new model, the batsman/keeper, in the Australian side. He made 159 in his first Test innings as an opening batsman. After Rod Marsh retired, Wayne opened the batting or batted in the top four and kept wickets so there was a lot of pressure on him in those days. He was the keeper in my first Test match and I will always remember him and love him for taking my first Test wicket, a catch off Dilip Vengsarkar, to contribute to my one for 123 off 38 overs. So I am forever grateful that he didn't drop it.

For a Test player to open the batting and keep wickets requires an extraordinary level of natural talent. This was at a time when the Australians were looking for extra batting power because we weren't going all that well. Wayne's willingness to potentially sacrifice his game for the good of the team led him to start keeping in One Day Internationals. Then the selectors took the next step in the Test side and realised that they could play an extra batsman if he played as a wicket-keeper in Tests too. He kept smoothly, he was fantastic in the slips or in the covers when he fielded, and he was a hard-hitting, quick-scoring left hand bat. That is a rare package.

Talented as he was, Wayne, along with Greg Ritchie, clashed with Bob Simpson on some of Bob's ideas for how the Australian side should move forward. Wayne was one of the last of the part-time, professional international cricketers. He showed what he would do for the benefit of the team by taking on the dual roles he did. He played the game because he loved it, but had to work outside cricket to make a living. He played at the top level because he was such a magnificently gifted player. The change of cricket to a full-time, professional job changed the nature of the game and Wayne's relationship with it. To me he was one of the last of the old school legends who played the game for the joy of it. His approach to playing the game was something I tried to follow.

Wayne N. Phillips

Tests
1 (1992), 22 runs (14)

First Class
60 (1988–1994), 3859 runs (205), 1 wicket (1 for 59), 24 catches

Wayne Phillips 2—'Rowdy'—the little bald-headed opening batsman from South Melbourne, was tough as nails. Have a look at his record for Victoria. For a very long time he was outstanding.

He got the opportunity to play one Test match. It was an unfortunate Test match for Wayne because the Western Australian hero, Geoff Marsh, got dropped for the Perth match and Wayne filled his spot. So he was never going to get any support from the WACA crowd. At one point, he chased the ball down to the boundary and threw it in. Some of the punters were giving it to him because they wanted Geoff in. He just turned around and flipped them the bird—and a camera was right there. It was a great shot.

That Perth Test was the last Test of the tour. The Australian side went to Sri Lanka after that, but opened with Tom Moody. If they were fair dinkum they should have taken Rowdy to Sri Lanka and given him the opportunity. Every few years a batsman gets thrown to the wolves and plays the one Test match, doesn't perform to his best and then gets spat out. It is usually because they are replacing an injured player with much higher credentials, and it is not really anything the player can control. Rowdy admits that he was almost embarrassed to be a Test player because he only played the one match. But no one should be embarrassed about playing for Australia.

He was small but he was a tough, competitive beast. He would take a certain amount of crap but when the crap pile got too high he turned nasty. I remember one day at Perth airport, we were flying home after a game and everyone was a little bit tired and emotional because we'd had a pretty heavy night the night before. We were sitting at the boarding gate and I started putting my middle finger and forefinger in each of his eyes and my thumb in his mouth. 'What are you doing?' he asked.

'I'm going ten pin bowling later on, I'm just trying you on for size.'

I got a short, sharp, right jab. 'Listen, big fella. Enough shit.'

I could tell that it was time to stop. Happy days.

Wayne was a great contributor to both South Melbourne, his club side, and also to Victorian cricket at state level. During the Sheffield Shield final for the 1990/91 season I was in the West Indies, and I rang Tony Dodemaide on the night of the third day's play. Victoria was two for 20 overnight, chasing 222 for victory. Dodders was confident we would win; he reckoned we wouldn't lose another wicket. We had Jamie Siddons and Rowdy batting and the ball had stopped swinging. I couldn't believe his confidence. The next day, Jamie Siddons got a hundred and then tried to manufacture a century for Rowdy. A century in a Shield final in the fourth innings is a career-defining achievement. Rowdy told Jamie to just get the runs. He wasn't after personal glory, he didn't want to flirt with the game. He ended up on 91 not out in 332 minutes.

That was Rowdy Phillips: team first and the individual didn't matter. He was an absolute ripper.

Greg Campbell

Tests

4 (1989–1990), 10 runs (6), 13 wickets (3 for 79), 1 catch

ODIs

12 (1989–1990), 6 runs (4 not out), 18 wickets (3 for 17), 4 catches

G reg Campbell: little upstart from Tasmania. There is no doubt about that. I used to look at him—at the way he would prance around—and think, I don't like this bloke at all. Then he got selected for the 1989 Ashes tour after taking 36 first-class wickets in the 1988/89 summer. He was my roommate during that tour and that's when I found out what a fantastic bloke he is.

His selection for the Ashes tour was a big surprise to most of us. He had only played twelve first-class games before he was picked. Geoff Lawson, Terry Alderman and Carl Rackemann were the three lead bowlers and Greg and I, on our first tour, were there if the selectors wanted to play four quicks. The plan was for Greg and I to spend time with Geoff Lawson and Terry Alderman to develop our bowling. Carl did his knee early in the tour so both Greg and I played the First Test in 1989 as part of a four-man pace attack. He didn't play for the rest of that trip because Trevor Hohns came in and bowled leg spin.

We spent a lot of time together on the tour and a lot of it was spent talking bowling with Lawson and Alderman. They made a big effort to give us as much guidance as they could, and Greg and I spent most of the time giving the old blokes a hard time. He had a sense of humour much like mine, so we thought we were pretty funny.

Greg wasn't the tallest bloke but had a really slick action and bowled with good bounce and good shape away from the right-hander. After the Ashes tour, he played three Tests over the 1989/90 summer and took 12 wickets. He was really looking like he would make it at Test level. Unfortunately he had a lot of bad luck with injuries and definitely should have played more Test matches than he did.

And he is Ricky Ponting's uncle, so is always going to be a handy name to know for trivia questions.

Damien Martyn

Tests

67 (1992–2006), 4406 runs (165), 2 wickets (1 for 0), 36 catches

ODIs

208 (1992–2006), 5346 runs (144 not out), 12 wickets (2 for 21), 69 catches

T20Is

4 (2005–2006), 120 runs (96), 1 catch

Damien Martyn came into the West Australian side as a youngster with a huge reputation for having a hell of a lot of talent, and for a long time 'potential' was a word that hung over his head. Ultimately, I think he lived up to his potential. When he got in, when he got his confidence up, he was a very good player. He was good off the front foot, particularly strong off the back foot. He had a beautiful back foot square drive that he played. I think he is one of the most graceful batsmen to have played for Australia.

He had a couple of things go wrong for him. The Sydney Test against South Africa in 1993/94 where Australia needed 117 to win in the second innings was a disaster for him. Damien was held responsible for the loss, but people forget he came in at five for 63 so he wasn't Robinson Crusoe in having a bad day with the bat. He hit one to cover, and was out caught with the score on 110. I don't think he was treated too well or too fairly after that and it was more than six years before he was selected again.

When he went back to the West Australian side he got a lot of grief because people said he looked like he wasn't putting in enough of an effort. That is the price of elegance, I reckon. When you have silky skills you will always look as though you're doing less than others. I also think that when an Australian player goes back to state cricket, everyone else steps up against them. I know as a young bloke, whenever we played against Queensland and Allan Border came in to bat, we wanted to be at our very best against him because we knew how good he was. That's what I think Damien went through.

I played under him when he captained the Australia A One Day International side in 1994/95, and he did a fantastic job. It's not too far-fetched to think that he could have captained Australia and done a very good job of that too. He was a great communicator. He was also a highly professional trainer. He took bowlers on in the nets the same way that he batted in the game. He was mentally tough, he had a fear factor of zero. Nothing worried him on the cricket ground. Whether he was going out to bat against spin, or against the fastest bowler in the world, he was unfazed. He backed himself. He was very good to have around.

He got back into the Test team after I had gone and he really had an impact. He was one of those guys who could turn a game. And I think the more mature he got the better he got. He was an outstanding cricketer playing in the Australian team with Ponting, Gilchrist, Hayden and Langer, and Damien Martyn was the player that I most liked to watch.

Craig McDermott

Tests

71 (1984–1996), 940 runs (42 not out), 291 wickets (8 for 97), 19 catches

ODIs

138 (1985–1996), 432 runs (37), 203 wickets (5 for 44), 27 catches

Craig McDermott in my opinion is the most underrated player to play Test cricket for Australia. He averaged well over four wickets per Test. His record is outstanding, he bowled a great shape, and I admire him for his courage and his character as well. The volume of overs he bowled—in a side that was more often than not up against a superior opposition—demonstrated that, as did his ability to come back so many times from injury. Volume of overs doesn't sound like a big deal, but try bowling 200 deliveries in 38 degree heat when you are the only experienced bowler in the team. His character was also tested because he had to come back after being dropped from the team several times.

He did have a lot of injuries throughout his career and that can be directly attributed to the amount of bowling that he did. I would see him in the rooms on the physio's bench looking in big trouble with crook knees or a sore back, and then he would come out and bowl the house down to win Test matches for Australia. He missed games at different times for what seemed to be superficial injuries, and copped flak for it.

But to bowl with him in a Test match was the highlight of my career, because when we were both on song, we could work a batsman over from both ends. I opened the bowling in more Test matches with him than with any other bowler. I always had an understanding of what he was trying to do to a batsman—pitch the ball up, swing it away—and my job was to push the batsman back by bowling short and trying to intimidate him. And I loved doing that!

Occasionally McDermott, who had a very good bouncer, would bowl to get the batsman on the back foot but predominantly he wanted him coming forward, playing at the ball on or around off stump so Craig could move the ball away.

When we talk about great Australian sides, and particularly great Australian sides in the last 30 years, people very rarely mention Craig McDermott. They go to players like Brett Lee, to Jason Gillespie, to Glenn McGrath, without fully understanding the impact that Craig had on the Australian side. In my opinion, on his day Craig McDermott could have been classed as one of the best bowlers in cricket.

Bruce Reid

Tests

27 (1985–1992), 93 runs (13), 113 wickets (7 for 51), 5 catches

ODIs

61 (1986–1992), 49 runs (10), 63 wickets (5 for 53), 6 catches

Some people may have heard Billy Birmingham's depiction of Tony Greig and Bill Lawry talking about Bruce Reid falling apart in his bowling action, with one arm falling off and his head rolling off his shoulders. And basically that's how Bruce Reid was. He was just held together by sticky tape most of the time. He was an outstanding bowler, but you wouldn't call him an outstanding athlete by any means.

For those who can't really remember Bruce, he was about 6 foot 7, might have been 6 foot 8, and, apparently, skinny. Side-on he looked like a rake with an Adam's apple. So it was hard to believe his body-fat testing results. In most of the testing that we did he had the highest body-fat percentage of anyone. Meaning, he didn't have any muscle to him. That probably explains why he got injured a lot of the time, because he put his body through hell—he bowled all day for you—and he was just skin and bones and a layer of fat as energy storage. His body couldn't take what he wanted to deliver—he simply wasn't strong enough.

But he was a very, very talented bowler. He averaged better than four wickets per Test in his 27 appearances for Australia, which puts him in the upper echelon of bowlers. He was a left armer, had the ability to bring the ball back in to the right hander, had steep bounce because he was so tall and he bowled at good pace. Cricket's not a game of ifs and buts, but if he had the build of Glenn McGrath, who had a fair bit of muscle on board—wiry, skinny but strong—if his body had held out, he could have easily been a 350-plus wicket taker for Australia.

Plus he's a good fella. The nicest fast bowler I've ever met. But on the ground he used his height and his bounce to make batsmen fear for their safety. Legend.

Greg Ritchie

Tests
30 (1982–1987), 1690 runs (146), 14 catches

ODIs
44 (1982–1987), 959 runs (84), 9 catches

Any teammate who plays in your first Test is special and Greg Ritchie was one of them. We played against India in December 1985, and he made a big hundred in the first innings when everyone except David Boon struggled a bit. Kapil Dev took eight in our first innings. I had played against Greg in the Sheffield Shield and knew he had a terrific eye, but that innings against Kapil Dev showed how talented he was: 128 runs in 389 minutes against some incredible swing bowling was a monumental effort. I would reckon it was the best innings Greg Ritchie ever played and it made a huge impression on me. He had made his Test debut at 22 and scored a century in his second Test, and I thought that if I could make it at Test level then we would be teammates for as long as my career lasted. The next time I was back in the team was the following summer and we played three Ashes Tests together, and that was it for Fat Cat.

As a batsman he was elegant and played all the shots. He wasn't hassled by pace, he hit the ball hard and was happy to take on a bowler by hitting the ball in the air. He was beautiful on the drive and punishing square of the wicket on both sides. He played 30 tests but only nine were at home and he never really settled into the Test line-up. Although he was one of the most naturally gifted sportsmen I ever saw, he suffered from being one of the last of the old school when cricket was becoming professional. He was also a very, very funny man.

He loved the game and thought a batsman's role was to make runs. He didn't do too well when Bob Simpson came in and the expectations on other aspects of the game, like fielding and fitness, started to increase. I think he had a few problems with abstract concepts like team rules and skin-fold testing. But he had a great approach towards batting, he was a very talented cricketer and in another time he would have played many more Test matches.

Shane Warne

Tests

145 (1992–2007), 3154 runs (99), 708 wickets (8 for 71), 125 catches

ODIs

194 (1993–2005), 1018 runs (55), 293 wickets (5 for 33), 80 catches

You could give Shane Warne a golf club and he would go out and hit a good ball. Badminton, table tennis—anything that he set his mind to, he would be successful at. He is that sort of bloke. If he was interested in what he was doing, he wanted to be the best at it and with cricket he was fantastic.

The other thing about Warnie that really impresses me is the self-confidence that he has, and has always had. Some people say that Shane Warne is the way he is now because of what he has done. But Warnie is exactly the same now as he was as a nineteen-year-old kid coming into the Victorian state squad. He was cocky, he was full of belief, but he wasn't arrogant by any means. He had a very healthy respect for traditional values and senior players.

Matthew Hayden tells a story about his first encounter with Warnie. The Victorian team was up in Queensland

and we had won the toss and were bowling and we walked onto the ground as a team. Shane Warne was twelfth man. Matthew and Trevor Barsby were opening for Queensland. As they walked across the dog track that used to run around the Gabba, Haydos looked over his shoulder and there was Shane, cigarette in hand, eating a toasted cheese sandwich with a can of Coke. Haydos said to Trevor, 'Have a look at that, as if that is going to go anywhere in cricket.' They both had a giggle and walked out. Haydos always reflects back on that first impression he had of Warnie: little fat bloke feeding his face.

No one could have imagined how successful Shane Warne was going to be. Everyone knew that he had a really good talent as a leg spinner but a lot of people doubted he would make it. When he first started he was even told by one of Victoria's ex-coaches that there was no room for leg spin bowlers in first-class cricket in Australia. As much as that coach looks like a goose now, he might have been right—it was just that no one had bowled leg spin like Shane Warne.

I played in his first Test, against India at the SCG. He was just a quiet kid in the corner. He was the same when he got into the Victorian team. He watched everything around him, and observed how senior players went about preparing and playing Test cricket. He still expressed himself with his sense of humour—and the longer he was in the team the more talkative he became—but wasn't overbearing. Yet he was always full of confidence in what he could do. That's a pretty tough balance to strike for a young bloke in Test cricket.

His first Test match showed what I love about Warnie. A lot of people get into him for not being very smart but, mate, he is a smart man. It's easy to come into Test cricket and make a hundred and take a five for, but it can set the bar high and result in high expectations every time you go out. Warnie bowled 45 overs and got one for 150. Ravi Shastri was the wicket Warnie got, but he wasn't Shane's first bunny. Caught Jones, bowled Warne for 206. A young Sachin Tendulkar was also particularly keen on his bowling. One for 150 in your first Test. A lot of people would come away and think, Am I good enough? He came away from that with no scars. Warnie just didn't doubt himself.

He played the next Test and took none for 78 for the match. He was dropped, then toured Sri Lanka and played the First Test and took none for 107 in the first innings and three for 11 to clean up the tail and get a victory for Australia by 16 runs. He played another Test without taking a wicket. At this stage, Warnie's Test career stats were four Tests, four for 386. Then we got to the Second Test of the West Indian tour at the MCG. Boxing Day Test. On the biggest of cricket's stages, against the best Test team in the world. Warnie, in front of his home crowd, took seven for 52 in the second innings to bowl Australia to victory.

We went on the 1993 Ashes tour together. At that stage I had a fair idea of what he was capable of doing but probably even then didn't think he would be able to do it on a consistent basis. Of course, A.B. had plans for every opposition player. One of our warm-up games was against Worcestershire. Graeme Hick was playing for them and A.B. had told Warnie not to get his bag of tricks out against Graeme because he was going to be playing in the Test series. Warnie was relatively new on the scene and jumping out of his skin, but the captain had told him leg spin only so that's what he did. Hick just slogged him. Got big runs. Warnie got hit and it hurt him that he couldn't get out his variety. But the English blokes would have gone away thinking there was no reason to fear the little rotund blond-headed leg spinner from Australia because he just threw the ball up and did what he was told to do.

In the First Test it was open slather. Warnie's first ball—thrown up, drifting away, pitched outside leg stump—hit the top of off stump. The margin for error in that delivery is tiny. How it didn't hit the front pad or back pad, how it didn't flick the bat, how it just hit off stump—it was just phenomenal. It was *phenomenal*.

Right from that very first Ashes ball in England—'The Mike Gatting Ball', 'The Ball of the Century', call it whatever you want to—England were worried. Mike Gatting was seen to be the best player of spin in the English team and for Warnie to bamboozle him as much as he did would have sent panic through the English dressing room. He took 34 wickets in six Tests and at times he bowled genuinely unplayable deliveries.

Most players, once they hit form early in their career, then go on to have a purple patch for the next twelve to eighteen months. Warnie's lasted twelve years.

The thing that still amazes me about Warnie is that he can't see what the fuss is about. He says, 'I'm just a cricketer,' and I think, Mate, you're probably just a little bit better than that. He doesn't see that. So I think that's a sign of a bloke who really enjoyed what he did for a long time and wants to get on with his life. He just marches to a different beat.

People who don't know him sometimes don't think too highly of Shane Warne. People who have met him and know him reasonably well just love him. You can't help but to love him. He is just fantastic. He is so full of enthusiasm, loves life and when you're around him he just lifts you up and gets you going. He is the quintessential lovable rogue.

Tim May

Tim May is a legend partly for the work he did as a player—he was, in his own right, a very, very good spin bowler for Australia (although, unfortunately for him, he was playing at the same time as Shane Warne, so found it hard to get a regular spot). He's also a legend for the work he did at the Australian Cricket Association. He is a very shrewd operator and he really gave the players a voice.

Maybe because of this, the perception of Tim by the general public is that he is a very serious, down to earth sort of a person. But the truth is, within the group he was a comic genius. Tim has a very wicked and different sense of humour and the ability to make anyone laugh at any time. He was one of the three stooges: Ian Healy, Steve Waugh and Tim May. If we won a Test match you would want to be around those three blokes.

Some of the things he did were absolutely stupid. I roomed with him on the 1989 Ashes tour and more than once I was woken up in the middle of the night by Maysie rattling around trying to find his anti-snore shirt. Apparently if he wore it to bed, he wouldn't snore. Bizarre.

But Maysie was a bit of a medical mystery because he could find injuries where no one else could. If anyone was going to get injured it was going to be him. In 1989 in England, in the nets at Lords, Tom Moody was having a whack and lifted the ball out towards the boys across the other side of the ground. The call went up, 'Look out, look out!' Everybody ducked their heads but Tim looked around and copped it in the face.

In 1993 we played an early game against Somerset. All tour we had all been getting into Maysie, calling him soft. If he got a little cut, a bruise or anything, he was a drama queen. At the start of the game he had calluses on his bowling fingers that were starting to blister over because he had been bowling a lot in the nets. He sat there gnawing away at these calluses until they were almost back to the bone and then he poured on Friar's Balsam. Now, if you put Friar's Balsam on an open wound, you get a bit of a hurry up. But Maysie did just that. The rest of us were just looking at him thinking, What's going on here? He gets a paper cut and he almost dies, but here he is almost gnawing a couple of his fingers off so he could rip the ball!

After that game, Somerset's off spinner comes in while we're having a beer, and he says to Maysie, 'You got the ball to turn. I've played here for four or five years and never turned the ball on that wicket. What's your secret?' Maysie shows him his fingers and tells him he had to grip the ball and really rip it so the seam cut his fingers to shreds. This bloke says, 'Oh, I don't want to do that!'

Another time, I was bowling to him in Adelaide and hit him in the hand, and must have broken a few bones. He got the glove off and his hand had just blown up—it looked like he had a cricket ball attached to the side of it. He was holding his arm and the South Australian physio has run out and looked at him. 'Where did it hit you, Maysie?' Maysie has just looked at him and said, 'On the elbow.' And the physio started working on his elbow! Maysie went crook at him and needless to say, the rest of us found it pretty funny.

For all the crap we gave Maysie, he was a tough man and a good bowler who knew how to enjoy his cricket.

Steve Waugh

Tests

168 (1985–2004), 10,927 runs (200), 92 wickets (5 for 28), 112 catches

ODIs

325 (1986–2002), 7569 runs (120 not out), 195 wickets (4 for 33), 111 catches

People who don't know Steve see him as the iceman with no emotion. I reckon he is a relaxed, laid-back, good bloke. He is also very talented and as mentally tough as anyone I played with.

I suppose Ian Chappell and Steve Waugh are the ugly brothers, compared to Greg Chappell and Mark Waugh. If you paid money to watch someone bat you would go and watch Mark and Greg because of their beautiful and effortless shot-making. If you wanted someone to bat for your life, you would pick Ian and Steve every time.

I can remember early in Steve's career it was said he looked very uncomfortable against quality fast short pitched bowling, early in his innings. Which batsman isn't? Not too many batsmen are able to get through that. Certainly Steve Waugh had the ability to cope with being struck by bowlers, to play and miss, knowing that he would get his chance to score against bad balls eventually. His record for Australia is outstanding and he took his game to another level when he took on the captaincy. And that's been the strength of Australian cricket: the strength of our captains from Ian Chappell to Allan Border to Mark Taylor and Steve Waugh.

When Steve had to bat with the tail, it was usually because we were in a tough situation, and this brought the best of his leadership qualities out. It was interesting to hear a lot of commentators say that he was very selfish because he used to bat for not outs. But batting with him as a tail ender just gave you the confidence to be able to bat. If we were playing the West Indies, Malcolm Marshall and Curtly Ambrose would be bowling and he would ask, 'Who do you feel comfortable against?'

Usually my response to that would be, 'Neither of them. Can you bat at both ends and only score even numbers?'

If we weren't playing the West Indies, there was usually one bowler that I was more comfortable facing, so Steve would try to let me face that one and he would take the other. He would be constantly encouraging a tailender: 'Don't do anything stupid. If the ball's there, hit it, but don't play any stupid shots. We can get some runs here.' That was his view; he didn't want to dominate the tail, he wanted to give you a little bit of rope and a lot of belief that you were as much a part of the partnership as he was.

I had the opportunity to bat with him at Headingley in the 1989 Ashes. Having been 22 yards away and watched the way that he hit the ball and how cleanly he hit it, I can tell you that you really don't get how hard he hit the ball from watching it on TV, or even from watching it from the boundary. But from 22 yards away, the way he could split the field was amazing. At one stage, England had a deep point, with a deep backward point 25 metres away, and Steve would hit the middle of them and get a boundary. They would move the point around to backward point and the backward point a little bit finer and he would split the two again! Then they would move a little bit forward and again he'd split them.

I first came across him as an opponent in Sheffield Shield matches. Playing against him, I quickly learnt that the harder you went at him, the taller he stood. So what we used to do was try to take the intensity out of the game. We wouldn't sledge him. We'd just try to keep everything as casual as possible. Because if you got stuck into him, that's when he used to lift. So we would just take the emotion out of it and try to almost make it like a social game. As his teammate, I used to love it when bowlers would go at him hard. You'd sit back and have a little grin on your face because you knew that was just going to make him more determined.

Our Test careers started in the same series, against India in Australia in 1985/86. Well, his started and mine stuttered. He was selected to play for Australia at the age of twenty. I played in the First Test and was twelfth man for the Second Test, Boxing Day at the MCG, when Steve made his debut. My first impression of him as a teammate was that he wasn't cocky but he was certainly very self-assured. He was definitely talented, he could bat, he could bowl and he was a tremendous fieldsman. But he was a long way from being the most talented player I saw. But he was so strong-willed, he understood his game, knew what his weaknesses were and worked tirelessly to eliminate them.

The more I played with him, the more I enjoyed his company. A Test victory was like popping a cork on Steve and his comic mates, Healy and May. When he captained Australia everyone seemed to think he was just so serious and really intense, but that's not the Steve Waugh that the blokes who played with him knew. He had a very casual yet determined air about him.

Steve Waugh was an outstanding player, with a lot of talent and a good bloke's sense of humour. He was a great team man and if you were stuck in the trenches, you would want Steve Waugh next to you.

Mike Whitney

Tests

12 (1981–1992), 68 runs (13), 39 wickets (7 for 27), 2 catches

ODIs

38 (1983–1993), 40 (9 not out), 46 (4 for 34), 11 catches

Mike Whitney always did everything flat out. He was a strong left armer, who was plucked from outside the squad to play the last two Test matches on Australia's 1981 Ashes tour. Six and a half years later, he returned to the Test team, played ten more Test matches and stuffed up one of the greatest trivia questions of all time.

He got seven wickets in an innings against India in Perth in the Test debut match for Paul Reiffel and Wayne Phillips 2. Whit was impressive because his best effort was an extraordinary seven for 27 and his worst effort would be one or two for 60 off 23 overs. So he was never far away. At the top level he may have lacked a bit of bounce and that's the only criticism that you could have pushed his way, so he was one of those blokes in that bracket: he was probably a couple of inches too short for the pace that he bowled or he was a couple of yards too slow for his height.

While he was playing, there were a lot of bowlers around—Carl Rackemann, Geoff Lawson, Craig McDermott, Bruce Reid, Paul Reiffel—a lot of guys vying for spots, so Whit was unlucky that he didn't play more Test matches.

Mike Whitney never took a backward step, gave his all with the ball, gave his all in the field. He couldn't bat but had himself convinced that he could, which is the main thing. Another thing about him was that it didn't matter who he was bowling to, if he had something to say, he'd say it. I always thought you had to pick and choose your battles. I think sometimes you've just got to bite your tongue, and that's coming from me! But he chose every batsman as a battle. He just loved the contest.

I love Mike and he's going to hate this story, but fast bowlers are renowned for not being that smart. One day we were in Tassie in the middle of a tour, and Mike got called in to cover an injury. Gets into the rooms, gets given his kit. Straight away he gets out his marker pen and starts writing on the label of the shirt. So I ask, 'What are you doing?'

He says, 'I'm writing my name on the tag, because you bastards will knock it off. I always lose shirts!'

I pick up his shirt and hold it up with the back of the shirt facing him. That's the side with 'WHITNEY' printed on it.

Up in Darwin one time, we went out fishing a fair way off shore and we came across a crescent moon shaped sandbar about 500 metres long. We'd been fishing inside one sweep of the sandbar. The boat runs up onto the sand and the skipper tells us there are no worries about crocs; nothing can eat us out here. We go for a swim. Mike, ever the explorer and outdoor adventure man, walks up one end of the crest, then walks up the other end and then he drops to his knees and yells at us to come and have a look at something.

He's found this little octopus and he is prodding it with his finger. The octopus is rearing up on his back legs, you can imagine it, looking really pissed off with Mike and not backing down. 'Have a look at this angry little fella,' says Mike.

'Listen, I'm no expert, Mike, but what sort of octopus do you think that is?' I ask him.

'I've got no idea.'

'Mike, when you poke him and he lights up, what colour are those rings on him?'

'They're blue, Merv.'

'What sort of octopus do you think it is, Mike?'

'Oh. Shit.'

Now, I don't know exactly what a blue ringed octopus does, I don't know how it stings you or bites you or how it injects you, but here's Mike sitting out on a sandbar, out of sight of land, prodding an angry little sea creature with his finger. A marine biologist he is not.

David Hookes

Tests

23 (1977–1985), 1306 runs (143 not out), 1 wicket (1 for 4), 12 catches

ODIs

39 (1977–1986), 826 runs (76), 1 wicket (1 for 2), 11 catches

David Hookes made his Test debut in the Centenary Test at the MCG in 1977. He joined World Series Cricket and then came back to the Test team. My first Test match was Hookesy's second-last. Hookesy was a very talented batsman, an aggressive cricketer with the bat and in the field, and loved to try the unusual if he thought it might give him an edge.

He had a great cricket brain. A lot of people play cricket and know the game, and a lot of people play cricket, know the game, and think inside the square that everybody else is in. Hookesy didn't know what a square was and didn't care.

Mate, he was a very, very smart cricketer and the things that he used to do were astounding. At the Adelaide Oval, South Australia versus Victoria, Hookesy was captain of South Australia and Dean Jones was batting for Victoria against Andrew Zesers. Andrew wasn't a pacey bowler by any means, but he did play two one dayers in Australia's 1987 World Cup victory. Another trivia question you can win with. Because Andrew was a slow–medium trundler, Deano was batting a yard out of his crease. The wicket-keeper would go up to the stumps, Jones would go back into his crease. So Hookesy came up with this plan: for the third ball to Dean, Andrew was to bowl it wide outside off stump. So, the wicket-keeper stands back, Deano faces up a yard outside the crease, Zesers does what his skipper asks. Deano makes a big deal of an extravagant leave, stands there looking at the bowler as if to say, 'Mate, bowl at the stumps, you're nowhere near it.' The wicket-keeper moves out of the way, David Hookes at first slip has taken the ball and thrown the stumps down. Dean Jones is run out. Now how do you think of that?

In a game between South Australia and New South Wales at the Adelaide Oval, a wicket had fallen at the end of an over. Greg Matthews has come on to bowl for New South Wales, and in those days the off spinners used to bowl down the side of the pitch to get their length and get their flight. Hookesy is leaning on his bat and Greg Matthews bowls two or three balls. When he bowls the next ball Hookesy just goes across and goes whack, hits it out of the ground.

'What are you doing?' the umpire says.

He replies, 'If he can practise bowling, can't I practise batting?' Beautiful.

Hookesy was brash and confident but had the ability to back up any mouthing off he did. And he did plenty.

Ricky Ponting

Tests
168 (1995–2012), 13,378 runs (257), 5 wickets (1 for 0), 196 catches

ODIs
375 (1995–2012), 13,704 runs (164), 3 wickets (1 for 12), 160 catches

T20Is
17 (2005–2009), 401 runs (98 not out), 8 catches

I always remember when Ricky started playing Shield cricket for Tasmania. He was seventeen. Initially he was a bit impatient and looked like a young bloke in a hurry. He had no fear coming in at that age and he played all the shots. He wasn't threatened by pace. He wasn't intimidated by the opposition. You just knew immediately that this bloke was going to be a good player.

I played a Chairman's XI game with him in Hobart in November 1994 and played Australia A one dayers with him in 1994/95. He had a good positive approach to the game and nothing fazed him. When he got into the Test team, in 1995 in Perth against the Sri Lankans, he hit them everywhere. Made 96. We all knew he was good.

It was intriguing to see him develop on and off the field. I think everyone has moments in their career that change them for the better and I think his moment was the night at Kings Cross when he got into a bit of a scuffle. He copped a lot of criticism for it. He got dropped from the Australian side. After that incident I don't think anyone thought that he was leadership material. But to his credit, he went back to Tasmania and he worked on all aspects of his game. He came back a better player and a more mature person. It was a test of character.

He developed an impressive set of skills: his demeanour, the way that he handled the press, the way that he trained. A lot of people used to think he was lucky because he used to throw the stumps down from cover. Well, you knew it wasn't luck if you watched the way that he trained. He would throw the stumps down nine out of ten times at training, and at full tilt. He'd train at 100 per cent, he was just full tilt all the time. Even later in his career when people were talking about him retiring, I saw that he was still the first onto the training track and he was last off it. I think he was strong tactically too. He had a firm grasp of what he was doing and what the team was trying to achieve.

He captained Australia in 77 Tests. Early in his captaincy, he had all the stars—McGrath, Gilchrist, Warne, Langer, Hayden, Martyn, Gillespie, Lee, Kasprowicz, Bichel—a side of fantastic players who could look after themselves, so he used to look after his game. It wouldn't matter who you were, when things were going bad you just threw the ball to McGrath or Warne and you knew one was going to block up an end and one was going to take a wicket. Whichever one it was didn't matter.

He took a lot from the senior players and that's what I reckon made him so good. When we lost all the super-stars it left him in the lurch a bit. I think he got frustrated because the team couldn't deliver as well on a plan as when McGrath and Warne were in the side. To lose those guys and try to gain the confidence in and of the players, I think that was pretty hard.

But he gave everyone a go. With the younger side, he had to spend more of his time on his team rather than his own game so he could get the best out of them. I was a selector for five years while he was captain and his leadership quali-ties really impressed me. I thought he demonstrated what a great leader he was because towards the end of his reign he sacrificed his own game to concentrate on developing the team.

That had a real impact on me, to see the quality of Ricky Ponting. In England in 2009 after the Test series, he took a couple of games off for a rest and Michael Clarke took his place. Clarke was younger and new to captaincy so was full of enthusiasm and energy, but when Ricky Ponting stepped back in I realised that Ponting by then was a complete leader. He was fantastic. Punter, one of the greats of the game.

Greg Matthews

Tests
33 (1983–1993), 1849 runs (130), 61 wickets (5 for 103), 17 catches

ODIs
59 (1984–1993), 619 runs (54), 57 wickets (3 for 27), 23 catches

A great cricket brain, and a great cricketer. In a time when Australia was looking for more batting options he certainly gave them one, batting anywhere from six to eight, often batting in front of the wicket-keeper. He was also a very good off spinner.

He took five wickets in the second innings of the tied Test in Madras in 1986/87, so he played a starring role in a rare happening in Test cricket. He played in some tough times for the Australian side but nevertheless, his figures in Test matches for Australia were pretty tidy. He was a victim of progress of the game in that when he got dropped for Tim May it was at a time when the Australian selectors thought we could beat the West Indies using two spin bowlers. Tim May was seen as the better off spinner and the batting options had strengthened so Greg's batting strength wasn't so critical. Tim May and Warnie bowled very well but we still didn't beat the West Indies.

To talk cricket with him is always enjoyable, although he does have a tendency to go off track! He loves the history of the game and loves statistics of the game and is very knowledgeable, and to listen to him on the radio when he talks cricket is absolutely fantastic.

Michael Slater

Tests
74 (1993–2001), 5312 runs (219), 1 wicket (1 for 4), 33 catches

ODIs
42 (1993–1997), 987 runs (73), 9 catches

Michael Slater came on board in 1993. He had been making a lot of runs for New South Wales and everyone knew how aggressive he was. He was always wanting to get on with the game, sometimes to his own detriment.

He would just as likely hit a four as he would leave one outside off stump from the opening over of a Test match. Sometimes he would get us off to a ripping start, other times he would work his way into innings. But he was always brutal on bad bowling—and brutal on good bowlers bowling not quite where they should. He had a big slash square on the off and a big cover drive. It didn't matter whether it was the first ball of the innings or whether he had got into an innings; if it was there to hit, he would hit it. Sometimes he got out and people thought, What's going on with Slats? But that's just the way that he was brought up and the way that he played.

On the 1993 Ashes tour, there was a real head-to-head between him and Matthew Hayden as to who was going to play in the international games. Hayden got the nod in the one dayers and Slats got the nod to make his debut in the First Test. It had been raining and there had been a lot of conjecture over the wicket and indecision about whether to bat or bowl. England won the toss and sent us in. So they were expecting to take some early wickets, and Slats was making his Test debut in the first Test of an Ashes series in England. There are not many situations in cricket with more pressure than that. He made 58 and an opening partnership of 128 with Tubby, who went on to make a hundred and virtually set the game up for Australia.

He hit the ball well and throughout 1993 was a terrific contributor to the team. He went on to bigger and better things after I stopped playing but ultimately the way he played brought about his downfall at selection. He kept going after the ball early in his innings and when it didn't come off, as an opener it looked bad and it was putting pressure on the other guys at the top of the list.

Then again, often he took on the bowling and it did come off. At times you thought that he could have been a little bit more patient, but if he was, we probably wouldn't have seen half the innings from Slats that people really remember.

Trevor Hohns

Tests

7 (1989), 136 runs (40), 17 wickets (3 for 59), 3 catches

Cracka had a fairly unusual career. He made his first-class debut in 1972 and made his Test debut in January 1989, against the West Indies. His Test career was over by the last Test of the 1989 Ashes tour, six Tests later. He went on the rebel tour to South Africa in 1985/86 and 1986/87, which put a hole in his prospects of playing more for Australia. He wasn't really expected to play that much on the 1989 Ashes tour but, apart from the First Test, he played in every Test match and had an impact each time. By the end of that tour, he was 35 years old; the selectors started looking to develop some younger spinners.

He was a real old-fashioned fighter and he made some handy runs batting at eight or nine, and was solid in the field. He bowled loopy leg spin. He bowled really well and got some big wickets at key times in 1989. Off the ground his quirky sense of humour made him a good tourist too.

Later he went on to be chairman of selectors for Australia and he was much criticised. People tend to attack the chairman of selectors rather than the selectors as a panel.

I couldn't understand the criticism that he got because he was in the role at the time when Australia was doing very well—virtually unbeatable—and he was still copping flak for picking bad sides. You have to think, What more as a selector do you need to do?

At the end of the day, he had a nineteen-year first-class career, took 288 first-class wickets, and will always be one of the players who won back the Ashes in England in 1989.

Michael Clarke

Tests*

105 (2004–), 8240 runs (329 not out), 31 wickets (6 for 9), 125 catches

ODIs*

236 (2003–), 7683 runs (130), 56 wickets (5 for 35), 100 catches

T20Is

34 (2005–2010), 488 runs (67), 6 wickets (1 for 2), 13 catches

A ripper. Whether you love or hate New South Wales cricket, you have to love their selection policy. Pick 'em young and give them every chance to become the best they can be. Michael Clarke is a product of that thinking. He got into the New South Wales team as a pup and grew into the player that he is today. A hundred on Test debut, great in the field, offers a little bit as a bowler. He averages more than 50 after 105 Test matches. They are figures of a highly accomplished player. You can see the impact that Bob Simpson has had on Australian cricket by looking at Michael Clarke.

He is always looking for ways to keep a game moving. He will take risks to give the team a chance for victory, but he seems to have the knack of not taking outrageous risks. In the First Test in Barbados in 2012, the West Indians made 449 in the first innings and he declared at nine down, 43 runs behind, one over after the drinks break in the middle session of Day Four. It surprised everyone and the West Indians were three down in no time, all out for 148 and Australia won the game. He also showed courage to declare at the Oval Test match in a rain-interrupted match. Although it nearly cost Australia the game, it was the only way they could win. He is prepared to risk sacrificing a game to have a chance to win and a lot of Test captains aren't that courageous.

His true impact on the game in Australia may be still to come. He now has a highly skilled outfit to steer. His knowledge and astute assessment of the balance of a game makes him potentially one of the best captains Australia has seen.

David Warner

Tests*
30 (2011–), 2467 runs (180), 4 wickets (2 for 45), 24 catches

ODIs*
42 (2009–), 1287 runs (163), 11 catches

T20Is*
51 (2009–), 1391 runs (90 not out), 28 catches

David Warner the pocket rocket. He is all muscle. If he were a fish he'd be a tuna. He's not tall but he's got biceps like most people's thighs and the bat speed that he generates is just awesome.

I was involved in his original selection in the Australian Twenty20 team. He hadn't come from nowhere, he had been playing very well in domestic Twenty20. Anyone who had seen him in the New South Wales Twenty20 team that season said we couldn't *not* pick him for Twenty20 International because he hit the ball so cleanly. It was like watching lightning and waiting for the thunder to come. He just hit the ball so hard.

Watching his international debut, making 89 off 43,

was one of the highlights of my cricket life. Listening to the punters around Victoria complaining about 'another New South Welshman in the Australian team' can get a bit tiring, especially as the only national selector from Victoria, so it was great to hear the whingers declare him a superstar after the game. At least in the Twenty20 galaxy. But he was always going to be more than just a Twenty20 player.

After his spectacular international debut, most people had him pigeon-holed as a Twenty20 and one day player. That might have been because he made his international debut in Twenty20 and One Day Internationals before he had played a first-class game for New South Wales. By the end of the 2014 Twenty20 World Cup he had played 123 matches in the three forms for Australia, and only seventeen four-day matches for New South Wales.

But I always thought he would make a top-class batsman. To me he plays a lot like Adam Gilchrist. He plays good cricket shots and puts some of them in the air. But he plays cricket shots. His off drive is a lofted off drive, but it is still an off drive. People who know cricket know how hard it is to loft a ball out of a fieldsman's reach and he does it too often for it to be luck.

The other thing I love about him is that he backs himself. His first Test century, in his second Test match, was on a bowler-friendly wicket against New Zealand where he played an innings that was out of character for him, but was based on his belief that he could stay in long enough to make runs. He defended, defended, defended—and then powerfully hit the bad ball. He carried his bat, making 123 of Australia's 233 in the second innings. His second Test century, against India, was a completely different affair. India batted first, were all out for 161 off 60 overs, and Dave Warner finished the first day's play not out on 104! He made 180 in that innings and his fellow opener, Ed Cowan, was the only other Aussie to make more than 30 runs. It was a difficult day for batsmen, but his belief in his ability to punish the bad ball is what makes him so special.

His pathway into the Australian Test team is unique in Australian cricket. But I think as the Twenty20 game grows, we are going to see other players follow it. They will have David Warner to thank for showing what is possible.

Damien Fleming

Tests

20 (1994–2001), 305 runs (71 not out), 75 wickets (5 for 30), 9 catches

ODIs

88 (1994–2001), 152 runs (29), 134 wickets (5 for 36), 14 catches

Foundation Member of the Fast Bowlers Cartel. Test Hat-Trick Club. Late Order Batsman in the Seventies Not Out Stranded by Lack of Partners on Way to Big Century Club. Flem and I have a few things in common.

Music is not one of them. When he first got into the Victorian state side he was the kid with the mullet from Noble Park and he was a bit different. He was ten years younger than me, and at the time we had nothing in common. He liked heavy metal—Def Leppard, Faith No More—and I was into Leo Sayer and ABBA. He used to get into me for my music and I used to scratch my head at his music.

In those days, he was eighteen and didn't have a licence so he would catch the train to the MCG to play for Victoria. I'd often find him carrying his bag along Brunton Avenue and I would stop in the middle of peak-hour traffic, flick the boot and make sure everyone tooting their horns got a good look at the bloke who was holding up the traffic.

I roomed with Flem for a long time and I took it upon myself to train him well and train him early. We flew to Perth for a match early on and in those days we would get off the plane and go straight to training. We'd finish about 1 p.m. then check in at the hotel about 1.30 p.m. We were sitting in our room, me on the king size and young Flem on his little single.

At one point I tell him, 'Flem, I think it's time you went to the shop downstairs and got me two chicken salad sand-wiches and a can of diet coke.'

'Why should I do that?'

'Well Flem, I'm the senior player and if I don't treat you like crap how are you going to know how to treat a young player when you're a senior player?'

'Good point, big fella. Yeah, no worries!' And off he goes.

He comes back with the order and as we have nothing else to do, we're watching TV. The volume seems to fade, so I ask, 'Flem, where's the remote?'

I get no reply so I look over and he has his earphones in and is nodding his head around so there's no point asking again. I get up and turn the TV up but by the time I get back to my bed, I can't hear it again. Flem's still there in his own little head-banging world so I get up and adjust it again. This happens four or five more times until I sneak a look over my shoulder while I'm at the TV. Flem's there, all concentration, using the remote to turn it down as I'm turning it up!

Flemmo was a true swing bowler, good pace, and a different type of bowler from most of the guys around that era. Mostly guys would hit the wicket hard and try to do a little bit off the pitch but Flem was a genuine swinger of the ball. He had a lovely action and long levers, which is a friendly way of saying he has long arms and long legs and is gangly . . . but he was a very talented cricketer. He suffered from bad shoulder injuries and came back from serious shoulder surgery, which was a testament to the steel will he hid under the jokes.

He also played in that unforgettable 1999 World Cup semi-final against South Africa where he took it upon himself to go against the team plan because Lance Klusener had taken fours from the first two deliveries of the last over and South Africa only needed one for victory. This was three years after Flem had bowled the last over in the 1996 semi-final to beat the West Indies. Two great examples of someone performing at his best when the pressure was at the most intense.

I reckon Flem was so good under pressure because I gave him such a hard time as a youngster in the Victorian team. One time, we were playing Tasmania in Launceston, Victoria batting, and we were all in the players' viewing area with not much happening. Flem was twelfth man.

'Flem, see that ice-cream van down the other end of the ground?'

'What do you want?'

'I want you to go down to that ice-cream van and I want you to get me a Golden Gaytime.'

'Why should I do that?'

'Because you're twelfth man.'

'Okay. Anyone else?' No interest from our teammates. I give him some money and he walks the length of the ground to the other end. We can see him from our seats, so we see him lean on the counter of the van, have a bit of a chat, then make his way back to us.

'There's no Golden Gaytimes,' he says. 'But they've got Choc Wedges.'

'Good. Did you get me one?' I ask.

'No.'

'You're an idiot.' I grab the money and walk around to the van at the other end of the ground. I get to the van and say, 'Mate, I'll have a Choc Wedge.'

He replies, 'We don't sell ice-creams.'

'What?'

'Your teammate was here five minutes ago, I told him we don't sell ice-creams.'

You know that feeling where you know everyone is laughing at you? I turn around and through the viewing glass in the room I can see the boys rolling around. Flem was a star.

PART

2

GROWING UP

Footy in the winter, cricket in the summer. I loved to watch
Australia playing Test cricket on the TV and then try to
emulate my favourite players in the Test matches fought
out in the backyard from October until March. I would try
to pick up mannerisms of technique and approach. How
a player talked, walked, chewed and spat. All critical
aspects of becoming like the legends who were
my heroes.

Harry Alexander

Tests

1 (1933), 17 runs (17 not out), 1 wicket (1 for 129)

Harry 'Bull' Alexander was heavily involved at the cricket and footy clubs in Euroa where Dad played. I was born in Euroa in 1961 and when I was six years old and found out that this bloke had played Test cricket, he was an instant hero. Fancy a bloke who had been to your house having been a Test cricketer! He was good mates with Dad, who was a very keen and pretty tough sportsman, and we were to and from Bull's place a fair bit. Bull was one of the first to write to me after I played my first Sheffield Shield match and continued to encourage me as I was trying to make my way in international cricket.

Bull had played one Test, the Fifth of the Bodyline series, in Sydney, in 1933. He was a big, strong, mean fast bowler and when Douglas Jardine accused him of running on the pitch and roughing it up, Bull decided to rough up Jardine as well. He aimed a barrage of bouncers at the English captain, landing more than one. This belated retaliation for Bodyline was loudly appreciated by the Sydney crowd.

Some of his teammates were Donald Bradman, Bill Woodfull, Victor Richardson, Bill O'Reilly and Stan McCabe. To me, he was a bigger legend than all of them.

W.G. Grace

Tests

22 (1880–1899), 1098 runs (170), 9 wickets (2 for 21), 39 catches

First Class

870 (1865–1908), 54,211 runs (344), 2809 wickets (10 for 49), 876 catches

Anyone who knows anything about cricket would know W.G. (William Gilbert) Grace. He intrigues me because of his legendary status. Although he only played 22 Tests, they were over twenty years. His first-class career tells the real story. He made his first-class debut at seventeen years of age and retired when he was 60. More than 54,000 first-class runs and 2809 wickets qualifies him as being a pretty fair all-rounder!

From my understanding he was a hard-nosed, tough competitor who knew how to entertain. Probably anyone who is hard-nosed and tough is going to get a mention in my list of legendary cricketers. Some people claim he is the man who made cricket into a spectator sport, because he could bludgeon the ball like nobody else.

I first heard of W.G. when I was pretty young. When I started playing senior cricket as a fourteen year old at

Buffalo, if ever there was an old bloke in the other side the comment was always, 'He would have played against W.G.'

Ian Chappell

Tests

75 (1964–1980), 5345 runs (196), 20 wickets (2 for 21), 105 catches

ODIs

16 (1971–1980), 673 runs (86), 2 wickets (2 for 14), 5 catches

As a boy in love with cricket, growing up in the sixties and seventies, I had three heroes who had an enormous impact on how I played the game. Ian Chappell, Dennis Lillee and Rod Marsh were three icons of the sport.

One of the things that I loved about Ian Chappell was his team leadership. He led by example and seemed to enjoy the contest more when he was against a strong opponent. The tougher the competition and the tougher the situation, the better he seemed to play. There were players who were more talented than him, but more determined and more courageous? I doubt it!

As a captain, he was fairly ruthless. He was a hard taskmaster and expected everyone to be able to do their job. With that, he was also very compassionate and really looked after his team. He was very much a player's man, always stuck up for his players. It was never him and the rest; it was always just about the team. So he got my vote every day of the week and as much as any individual, he is responsible for setting the template for how successful Australian teams play the game.

As a young bloke growing up, I played cricket in the backyard with my mates, and every time I batted I tried to be Ian Chappell: I'd have the collar up, I'd be chewing the gum, I just wanted to play a pull or hook shot every ball. Didn't matter whether it was a yorker or a full-length ball, I'd still be trying to play a pull or a hook because that's what Ian Chappell did. I suppose I'd chip off at the opposition as well because that's what Ian Chappell did too.

'Chappelli' played in the first One Day International, against England at the MCG in 1971 after a Test match had been washed out. He was also captain of the Australian team when it signed up for World Series Cricket, and after the truce, he returned for three Ashes Tests with his brother Greg as captain.

As a batsman, in his prime he was regarded as one of the best players of spin in the world. In difficult batting conditions he was second to none. And everyone knew that he loved the hook shot. It brought him undone a few times but his theory was that he made far too many runs with the hook shot so he wouldn't give it away. In the 1968/69 series against the great West Indies side, when everyone was talking about how fast and furious Charlie Griffith was bowling, to watch him just hooking and pulling the ball was a great inspiration for me. He is up there as one of my highest rated players of all time. He is an absolute champion.

Dennis Lillee

Tests
70 (1971–1984), 905 runs (73 not out), 355 wickets (7 for 83), 23 catches

ODIs
63 (1972–1983), 240 (42 not out), 103 wickets (5 for 34), 10 catches

Dennis Lillee was one of the greatest bowlers in the history of the game. When he retired, his 355 Test wickets was a record. He averaged more than five wickets per Test, and that is a good measure to use when trying to compare one bowler with another. But when you are talking statistics you need to consider his 24 wickets for Australia in matches against the Rest of the World and the 79 wickets he took in fifteen Supertests during World Series Cricket. That's 458 wickets in 89 Tests. The other thing to consider when you look at his statistics is that he had a bad back injury and spent time out of the game recovering and then modifying his technique. He was able to refine his action after the injury and become more efficient with everything he did.

When he first came into the game he was just a tearaway quick. When I was a young bloke watching him run in and bowl, he looked like he was all arms and fury. He had a lot of things going wrong with his action but his run-up was slick. He took five for 84 in his first innings as a Test bowler, against England in Adelaide, and he did what a top line bowler should: knocked over one of the openers, got the dangerous wicket-keeper/batsman and then cleaned up the tail.

In the Centenary Test in 1977, he took six for 26 in thirteen overs in the first innings and England were all out for 95. Then in the second innings, after the pitch had flattened out, he took five for 139 off 35 overs. That tells you that he had the capacity to be effective in any conditions.

He was aggressive, very fast and had a bucket load of variation. When he had a good day, he had a really good day. Some of his figures for a match or for a spell were remarkable and watching him play was an inspiration to a young cricket fan.

Growing up watching Dennis didn't have an impact on my bowling action, but he had a huge impact on how I played the game. I loved his attitude that you're never out of the game until it's over. If Australia went out in the second innings with the opposition team needing 30 runs to win, Dennis would charge in like they needed 250 runs to win. I probably took on board that never-say-die attitude, no matter what the situation of the game was. In my eyes, he was the greatest bowler of all time.

Rod Marsh

Tests
96 (1970–1984), 3633 runs (132), 343 catches, 12 stumpings

ODIs
92 (1971–1984), 1225 runs (66), 120 catches, 4 stumpings

There is no show without Punch and if you are brave enough to call Dennis Lillee Judy, then certainly Rod Marsh was Punch! He was a record-breaking wicket-keeper and was as tough as nails. 'Caught Marsh, bowled Lillee!' was the catchcry of my backyard cricket life. With Rod keeping to the blistering pace of Jeff Thomson and the guile and aggression of Dennis Lillee, and with Ian Chappell standing beside him at first slip, who would have wanted to be an opposition batsman?

He was an aggressive, talkative, combative player. How I wish they had stump microphones in those days. Watching on the black and white you couldn't hear what he was saying, but you could always see his gob going up and down under his moustache. You didn't know whether he was having a go at the batsman or encouraging his team-mates, but whatever it was, he was always talking behind the stumps. All I know is that if I could have heard him, I am sure I would have learnt a few words my mother didn't teach me.

He wasn't the prettiest batsman to watch, but he was certainly effective. Marsh was the first Australian wicket-keeper to make a Test hundred and showed the importance of a wicket-keeper being able to bat and do a job with a batsman, or bat with the tail. He created the model of the wicket-keeper/batsman that successful Australian teams have refined with players like Ian Healy, Adam Gilchrist and Brad Haddin.

I suppose from a cricketing point of view the wicket-keeper is the yardstick of any team. If the wicket-keeper is dragging his backside along then the rest of the team will be too. Rod in any situation always looked aggressive and positive. He loved testing, difficult conditions in a game and they brought the best out of him. He loved a contest, loved the fight, and that's what made the Australian side so strong: they had a heap of blokes who just played for that contest, and Rod Marsh was a critical part of that.

Sam Gannon

Tests

3 (1977–1978), 3 runs (3 not out), 11 wickets (4 for 77), 3 catches

'Sam' Gannon was a left-arm quick from Western Australia. He played his first game for WA in 1966, but struggled to get a regular game—try getting a spot in an attack with Graham McKenzie (60 Tests), Ian Brayshaw (172 first-class wickets, Jamie's father), Dennis Lillee, Bob Massie and Terry Alderman. All the superstars going to World Series Cricket gave an opportunity to lots of young blokes to play Test cricket who otherwise wouldn't have played, and it helped some old blokes too! He played his first Test match in the 1977/78 series against India at the age of 30.

I was sixteen at the time, watching him on TV, and he got me with his attitude towards the game. He was a hustling, bustling bowler. He asked questions of batsmen and gave his all. He took seven wickets in his first Test, but only played two more. I was shattered when he was dropped because when I played cricket in the park with my mates I used to try to bowl left armed so I could be like Sammy Gannon!

A short career, but he had a huge impact on me. I

suppose when I think about how I played the game, you could say my approach of trying to impose myself on batsmen both physically and mentally is a reflection of how I saw Sam Gannon.

Clive Lloyd

Tests
110 (1966–1985), 7515 runs (242 not out), 10 wickets (2 for 13), 70 catches

ODIs
87 (1973–1985), 1977 runs (102), 8 wickets (2 for 4), 39 catches

If I could be anyone in the world I would be Clive Lloyd. He was the most successful captain of the West Indies at the end of his career. His captaincy produced the beginning of the era of dominance by the West Indians. One of the notable things he did, after playing and losing against Lillee and Thomson, was creating the four fast bowler strategy. He was a great leader who developed a sense of professionalism in the players from the different countries that make up the West Indies.

A cousin of Lance Gibbs, the spin bowler, Clive was also a fantastic player. I used to love his cover drive. He would get on the front foot and play the most beautiful, free-flowing, left-handed cover drive. And he would belt the ball. He was a big bloke, 6 foot 4, 6 foot 5, and laconic. Just seemed to lope around the field but if the ball came near him in the air, he would pounce. He looked like he was made of rubber, he was that loose.

I never got to play against him but did get to meet him. He was the team manager out here in 1988/89 and after the Test match in Perth when Geoff Lawson got his jaw broken, I was asked to play in the Prime Minister's XI game. At the function before the game Clive Lloyd said that West Indians never wear helmets but after watching Big Bird bowl in Perth he would always want to wear one. I thought, There'd be no use for him ever wearing a helmet against me because I would just be bowling half volleys outside off stump to see his cover drive!

Joel Garner

Tests			
58 (1977–1987), 672 runs (60), 259 wickets (6 for 56), 42 catches			

ODIs			
98 (1977–1987), 239 runs (37), 146 wickets (5 for 31), 30 catches			

In the World Series Cricket days I would go out to VFL Park to watch the day/night games. At the end of the game we would all run onto the ground and at that stage of my life I was eighteen, playing footy for Werribee in the VFA, key position, sometimes in the ruck, so I thought I was pretty big and powerful like a lot of overgrown eighteen year olds. I ran onto the ground and found myself very close to Joel Garner, and I reckon I came up to his shoulder! He was just huge. Six foot eight.

I used to just sit back and love watching him bowl. I loved the way he used to gather himself when he ran in. He would start hunched up and as he got closer to the bowling crease he would stand up, and he must have been an intimidating, imposing man to face. A massive, massive man, and according to A.B. and Boonie, he was the quickest that they faced.

He was the quintessential big quick. He'd bowl back of length and then he would slip in a yorker. Coming down from that height they would have been very hard for the batsmen to pick up. He was a great death bowler in one dayers because of his yorker. He took five for 38 in the 1979 World Cup Final.

He was a very good player for the West Indies for a long time. It was at a time when if the West Indies beat Australia, I didn't mind too much. The West Indies had a magnificent side. There was so much about the West Indian side that I used to love: Viv Richards, Clive Lloyd, Andy Roberts, Colin Croft, Wayne Daniel, but in particular Joel Garner.

Bob Willis

Tests

90 (1971–1984), 840 runs (28 not out), 325 wickets (8 for 43), 39 catches

ODIs

64 (1973–1984), 83 runs (24), 80 wickets (4 for 11), 22 catches

Bobby Willis, the big goose. In a radio interview Andrew Flintoff asked me who my favourite English cricketer was, and when I said Bob Willis he laughed at me. When I was young, watching Ian Chappell, Rod Marsh and Dennis Lillee, we saw a really good era of cricket and England was the mortal enemy. Of the English players at that time Bob Willis captured my imagination because of his effort. I used to love the way that he would run in and bowl, looking like he was wiping his backside with his bowling hand. Then he would arch out to the left and straighten up again for some reason, and I found that very amusing. When we played cricket in the park, if I had lost the toss and had to be England, every time I bowled I was Bob Willis.

Colin Croft

Tests

27 (1977–1982), 158 runs (33), 125 wickets, (8 for 29), 8 catches

ODIs

19 (1977–1981), 18 runs (8), 30 wickets (6 for 15), 1 catch

Colin Croft. The intelligent fast bowler. He's got degrees in everything. Got an airline pilot's licence. He is just making all the rest of us fast bowlers look bad, doing that sort of thing. He was another international player I grew up watching play who had a big impact on me.

He had a straight run-up that would be directly behind the umpire, so batsmen didn't see him until the last minute. Then he would swing out and be really chest-on with his front foot splayed wide on the crease. If I lost the toss in the backyard and had to be the West Indies, Colin Croft was the one I bowled as. Splay that front foot out, just big chest-on action.

I always found it intriguing to watch him bowl because he went against everything that you learnt about bowling. We were always told that the better batsmen would score easily if you bowled on an angle from wide outside off stump, but the better batsmen just seemed to struggle with him. I think they were worried about losing their head, not their wicket! He was a big man with strength, pace and accurate bounce. He was also able to bowl with an upright seam and was able to straighten the ball when bowling from that angle. His 125 Test wickets puts him well over the four wickets per Test benchmark, and shows what a quality bowler he was.

I faced him in a testimonial game at the MCG and he was a handful. He'd just angle in and cut the ball away. I would be getting ready to get hit and the ball would beat the outside edge. How he did it I have no idea. I said to A.B., who I was batting with, 'How good is this bloke!'

'Try about twenty years ago when he was bowling about 100 mile an hour quicker and see how you go,' came the answer.

He was rated really highly by the blokes that played against him and that is a measure of a player's quality.

Michael Holding

Tests
60 (1975–1987), 910 runs (73), 249 wickets (8 for 92), 22 catches

ODIs
102 (1976–1987), 282 runs (64), 142 wickets (5 for 26), 30 catches

Whispering Death. We had a young bloke trying to be a fast bowler at Footscray. Tony Dodemaide used to call the young fella 'Whispering Heartburn'. Dodders thought if the young bloke hit you, he wasn't going to kill you like Michael Holding. He would just upset you a little bit.

Most blokes make a bit of noise when they run in. They reckon Michael floated. His run-up was very long and very straight and he had his head going from side to side and his arms pumping through and he took a great delivery stride and bowled heat. But he was so light on his feet that the non-striker had to be watching because you wouldn't hear him.

He doesn't look like a big bloke, but he is so well proportioned he might be taller than I think. He was certainly lean. The pace that he generated was extraordinary because he was a pure athlete. He averaged more than four wickets per Test, and once took fourteen in a match. Growing up I loved watching him bowl. I watched him on television bowling in Perth to Ian Chappell, one of my favourite players of all time. It was Holding's second Test and this young bloke was sticking it up Ian Chappell and Chappell was giving as good as he got. Chappell made a heap of runs, but in the end Holding bowled him and I thought, Michael Holding will be one for the ages.

Doug Walters

Tests

74 (1965–1981), 5357 runs (250), 49 wickets (5 for 66), 43 catches

ODIs

28 (1971–1981), 513 runs (59), 4 wickets (2 for 24), 10 catches

Dougie Walters is a legend. Obviously I didn't play with him, but I will always remember the 1974/75 summer and the six he hit on the last ball of the day off Bob Willis in Perth to score a hundred in a session. He got a century in a session three times, and he scored hundreds in his first two Tests. He also was the first player to score a century and a double century in the same Test, against the West Indies in Sydney in 1968/69. He was clearly a natural and so had these runs of fine form.

Growing up, I used to love how Ian Chappell would throw Dougie the ball every time Australia couldn't get a wicket. Doug would come on and bowl a couple of overs and get a wicket and then get taken off again. That was his role. Partnership breaker. He bowled little swingers and little seamers, and was a great fieldsman.

He used to do Max Walker coaching clinics up in

Kilmore and I would do some coaching between matches. One day during one of these clinics I walked into a pub with Kerry O'Keeffe. Kerry just looks around and points at a corner and says, 'We're down there.' It's a Thursday night, pay night, and the pub's pretty full. I can't recognise anyone because the place is so crowded.

'How do you know?' I ask.

'Just look for the most smoke in the room.'

The corner he's pointed to looks like the Apaches are sending up smoke signals. We make our way to the corner and there is Doug Walters. Denis Hickey is sitting there reading out the clues to a crossword puzzle and writing down the answers. Kerry looks at me and says, 'Denis thinks he's joining in with Doug to do the crossword puzzle, but if Denis wasn't doing the reading and the writing, Doug would have to put down both his beer and his cigarette to do it, so he wouldn't do it at all!'

At another of Max's camps there were a few Victorian players: Tony Dodemaide, Simon Davis, Simon O'Donnell, Denis Hickey and me. Because we were missing training and staying up at Kilmore we had to do a fitness test and give the results to our conditioning bloke when we got back to Melbourne.

It comes time to do the fifteen minute run so off around the 400 metre track we go. Doug is sitting there, puffing on a cigarette with a beer in his hand, watching us go around and around. Then we have to do a minute of sit-ups and maximum push-ups, and the sit-and-reach test. At the end of the task Dougie comes over and takes a long pull on his smoke. 'You blokes are playing cricket, aren't ya?'

'What did you blokes do in your day?' someone asks.

'Used to bat and bowl.'

Life was simple then, wasn't it, and I can see how it suited Doug. To him, nothing is a problem. He's has a very even demeanour and he is happy letting life wash over him.

He was a wonderful batsman who made the game look easy. And that is how he lives his life.

Len Pascoe

Tests
14 (1977–1982), 106 runs (30 not out), 64 wickets (5 for 59), 2 catches

ODIs
29 (1977–1982), 39 runs (15 not out), 53 wickets (5 for 30), 6 catches

I used to love Lenny growing up; he's just mad. I reckon my earliest memory of Lenny Pascoe is in a Test match in Sydney, against India in 1980/81. We were on an Under-23s trip for Victoria down to Tasmania and we were watching it on the television but we didn't have the commentary turned on so we could listen to some music on the radio. Lenny was first change bowler to Dennis Lillee and Rodney Hogg, and Sandeep Patil was batting and doing a good job.

Then Lenny has drilled him. Patil had a helmet on, but the ball has got inside the visor and he's hit the deck. At that very moment, the song that happened to be on the radio was the Queen song 'Another One Bites the Dust'. The boys went berserk. Blokes that played against Lenny have since told me that he used to intentionally try to hit batsmen in the head. I would never condone violence in cricket, but it was a very good bouncer.

But apart from that, Lenny was extraordinary. He was a big strong bloke and he'd bustle in and bowl the ball as fast as he could. Got in the right area often enough and took four and a half wickets per Test. I wouldn't say he was the most naturally gifted person that played Test cricket but he worked his butt off and I reckon got every ounce out of himself. I just loved watching him. Loved watching him.

Gary Gilmour

Tests

15 (1973–1977), 483 runs (101), 54 wickets (6 for 85), 8 catches

ODIs

5 (1974–1975), 42 runs (28 not out), 16 wickets (6 for 14), 2 catches

Gus Gilmour was a left-handed all-rounder. He just tonked it when he batted and swung it when he bowled. He was a first or second change bowler and could swing the ball back in to the right hander. He had a heap of natural talent and could change the path of a game with bat or ball. He had a smooth, arcing run-up and when he hit the crease, the ball was delivered with a flurry of arms and he lost no pace through the crease. As well as being hugely talented, you could tell by the look of him, with his shirt tucked in tight, that he didn't mind the essentials of life: food and drink. He may have been the last Test cricketer unavailable for selection because of gout. He joined World Series Cricket in 1977 and didn't make it back to Test cricket after the truce. I watched him a lot as a young bloke and in the backyard I used to run in and bowl my Gus Gilmours, the left-arm mediums, just to change it up if I couldn't get anyone out, because he always seemed to take important wickets. When I was young, he inspired the way I approached the game. I have very fond memories of a bloke who was always having a crack.

Jeff Thomson

Tests
51 (1972–1985), 679 runs (49), 200 wickets (6 for 46), 20 catches

ODIs
50 (1975–1985), 181 runs (21), 55 wickets (4 for 67), 9 catches

'Ashes to Ashes, dust to dust, if Lillee don't get ya, Thommo must!' was a big cry for a long while in cricket crowds. Jeff Thomson took 200 Test wickets, despite interruptions to his career through injuries and two seasons with World Series Cricket.

He had a wonderful slinging action. I think if he was coming through today, with the way that guys are coached these days, he'd be told to start again. That's the thing about someone with a unique action. Bowling with the traditional well-coached action can make you a very good bowler, but to be really exceptional, you have to be a bit different. Growing up I just loved watching him bowl.

When you ask former players what batting against Thommo was like, the first reaction you get is raised eyebrows, followed by rolled eyes, and then some of them go a little pale. He got incredible bounce off the wicket for someone not much more than 6 foot tall. Extreme pace and bounce meant he had the ability to hit you in the throat off a good length, or break your toe. Because of that and his 'hard seeing' action where he used to curl the hand behind his back, he was a scary proposition.

Perhaps because of Thommo's almost mythical powers, there are a few stories about him that no one will verify. He played club cricket at Bankstown, with Len Pascoe. 'They' reckon that one day he bowled 'six byes'. The ball was a bit short, went through the batsman, over the wicket-keeper and hit the sight screen on the full. Not sure what the umpire's signal would be for that. Three arms in the air? 'They' also reckon that if the surf was good every club wanted to play Bankstown that week because Thommo and Lenny wouldn't turn up; they'd have gone surfing. The other side of that coin was that if the surf was bad, Thommo and Lenny would play but have the shits, so batting was even more dangerous than usual.

Another legend about the legend is the reason why, when he played at the Gabba, he always bowled from the same end. In the seventies the Gabba was nowhere near as developed as it is now and from the playing field you could get views of surrounding buildings and streets. From the top of his mark, Thommo could even see the local primary school with a pair of huge Moreton Bay fig trees to provide shade for the kids. One year he gets there for the first game of the season and is walking to the top of his run-up at the start of his first over. The field is set and the batsman faces up and everyone looks at Thommo. He's standing there, looking towards the boundary. He's obviously looking around for something, distracted. Nothing happens. Eventually Greg Chappell jogs up to him from slip.

'Thommo, what are you doing?' he asks.

'They chopped the Moreton Bays down.'

'Yeah, well, it happens, the price of living in a modern city. But we've got a game to play. You need to bowl.'

'Can't.'

'Why not?'

'They've chopped the fig trees down. Don't know where my run-up is.'

Jeff Thomson was a one-off. His unconventional technique wreaked havoc through Test batting orders around the world and took Australia to the top of cricket in the 1970s. A genuine legend.

Alan Thomson

Tests

4 (1970–1971), 22 runs (12 not out), 12 wickets (3 for 79)

ODIs

1 (1971), 0 runs, 1 wicket (1 for 22)

First Class

44 (1968–1975), 260 runs (34 not out), 184 wickets (8 for 87), 12 catches

We used to watch Froggy Thomson in the Shield matches we went to and I was mesmerised by his action. He is another Test player who would not get through the development system these days. He was a medium–fast right-arm bowler whose delivery stride was a skip, and he ended up delivering the ball with a windmill action with his right foot as his front foot. It looked as bad as it sounds. He did all that and still got the ball in the right spot, bowled good pace and had the ability to swing the ball both ways. It must have been effective, because he got his first 100 wickets for Victoria in less than twenty games. He couldn't quite break through to consolidate a Test position and his last Test was Dennis Lillee's first. Bad timing, Froggy.

But he was another unique cricketer who was around in the seventies and showed that looking technically correct didn't matter, if you were effective. Which is why I didn't worry too much when some smart-arse described my run-up as making me look like a stiletto-wearing furniture removalist trying to get a fridge through a doorway.

Max Walker

Tests
34 (1972–1977), 586 runs (78 not out), 138 wickets (8 for 143), 12 catches

ODIs
17 (1974–1981), 79 runs (20), 20 wickets (4 for 19), 6 catches

Got to love big Maxy for his heart and soul. If you've ever had anything to do with Max Walker you just love him.

He came across from Tassie to play football for Melbourne and ended up playing Test cricket. He bowled a mountain of overs and was a really good foil for Dennis Lillee and Jeff Thomson. Some of his best performances were when Lillee or Thomson, or both, were absent from the team. He took eight for 143 in the MCG Ashes Test in 1974/75 and took 26 wickets in the tour to the West Indies when Dennis Lillee was injured. Max could swing the ball in just about any conditions, got movement off the seam, and had a very awkward looking, disjointed action that was halfway between Froggy Thomson and normal.

I got into the state squad when he was getting towards the end of his career. Training with him, he always had something to say to a young bloke. He was great. He'd give you a pat on the back. He always said hello. As a senior player, he didn't have to do it. But he looked like he wanted to give you a hug every time he saw you. He is that sort of a bloke.

I've had a lot to do with him over the years and regularly someone will come up to me to talk about a sportsman's night that they'd been at in the late seventies and how much they'd enjoyed it and how good I'd been as a guest.

'Not me, Max Walker,' I'll reply.

'Yeah, that's right, you. Max Walker.'

Both of us played in a charity game against the Dalai Lama XI in the mid-nineties. Seriously. The Dalai Lama XI. I'm just standing there when a bloke walks up to me and stands a foot away from me, no sensitivity for personal space.

'Big Maxy! Ah I love ya, you used to run in and bowl . . .' and he's doing all the arm actions and carrying on about me being Tangles.

I look up and say, 'Mate, I'm not Max Walker.'

'Ah don't muck me around mate. You're Max Walker.'

'Mate, I'm not Max Walker.'

He looks at me and says, 'You're Max.'

I say, 'Mate, I'm not Max Walker. I'll prove it to you.'

'How you going to do that?'

'Because this is Max Walker standing next to me!'

The guy looks at me and looks at Max, looks at me, looks at Max. Jumps across in front of Max, puts his face a foot from Max's and goes into the spiel again!

After he's gone we have a laugh about how often Max gets called Merv. Soon after that, I walk into the airport and spot Max halfway up the escalator on his way to the Qantas Club lounge. So I shout up at him, 'Merv, Merv! Hey, Merv!' I see him drop his head and shake it and then turn around. When he sees me this big booming smile breaks out. He's just a loveable bloke, Maxy. He's fantastic.

PART

3

LEARNING TO PLAY THE GAME

As much as Test heroes inspire you to dream, it is the
people you meet along the way that have the greatest
influence on how far you go in the game. The journey to
the Test team means going through different levels of
competition. Every level requires new skills and different
preparation. I don't know when I first learnt about
sledging, but I am sure it was from a teammate. Coaches
drill you in the technicalities and the physical preparation.
Senior players show you what is expected in terms of
mental preparation, how to think about the game and how
to stay out of trouble in pubs. Teammates teach you about
life and character and why we play this testing, difficult
game. And often, opponents teach you about courage and

although at the time you would do anything to give them
a bad day, you know that you would love to have them on
your team. To become a Test cricketer, I depended on
a lot of people who helped me because of their love
for the game.

Robert Steer

I think anyone who has played competitive cricket as a young bloke is inspired by someone they played with who's a little bit older. For me, that was Robert Steer.

I first started playing senior cricket as a fourteen year old for Buffalo Cricket Club at Myrtleford in the Ovens Valley, in the same team as my dad. Robert was the captain of the team. He was everything that I wanted to be as a cricketer. He was big, rugged, tough and a great player. New ball bowler, number three and number four batsman. He could field, he could stand at first slip. If he went into the outfield, he would always take a catch somewhere. He'd get a run out. As if that wasn't enough, he also played football in the local league! He was just a superstar.

Growing up with Dad, I used to go in to training with him a lot. Anyone who's played country cricket would understand that the training is not all that intense. Nevertheless, I used to just sit back and watch the way that blokes used to go about it. It wasn't long before I cottoned on to what the better players did, and they always seemed to train just a little bit better than most. It might not have been harder, it might not have been longer, but for some reason it was just better.

For example, I reckon every time Rob Steer picked up the ball in training he bowled at the stumps. You might think, Well that's a novel idea isn't it, bowling at the stumps every time? But that's what he did, and he just played the way that he trained. In the nets he would get in and bat and then he would start hitting the ball. Just as he would build an innings when he was playing. So it wasn't about hitting the ball from ball one.

When you've got blokes like that around you, you learn from them constantly. I used to hang off every word he uttered and I learnt a lot from what he said, but I learnt even more from what he did and how he stood up. He was my hero for a few years: Robert Steer, the king of cricket.

Steven Feltsted

Up at Myrtleford, Steve played for the Myrtleford Rovers, which were our team's arch enemies. When I was about sixteen years old he was twenty and he was the captain of my Under-21 Colts side, so he was someone I looked up to. He was another all-rounder and, like all good leaders, led by example. As captain and middle-order batsman, he always seemed to be the one to bowl and to get runs during tough times.

He has a really good cricket brain. We occasionally still catch up, and I enjoy talking cricket with him. He says he hasn't got his finger on the pulse but when he talks about the Australian or the Victorian team he always manages to make me sit back and think, Shit, what he says makes sense. There are some blokes who just have an eye for cricket.

You can't overestimate the contribution both Steve and Steery made to my development and to understanding what was needed to get the best out of myself. When you're playing rep cricket at under 21 there are a lot of talented players. But these two blokes showed me that it's not about how talented you are, it's about how well you do in pressure situations. There's nothing flashy about it: it's all about hard work. That was a good lesson to learn.

Ron Gaunt

Tests

3 (1958–1964), 6 runs (3), 7 wickets (3 for 53), 1 catch

First Class

85 (1955–1964), 616 runs (32 not out), 266 wickets (7 for 104), 31 catches

Pappy Gaunt. A few decisions are made for you in life and my decision to become a fast bowler was not my own. It was Ron Gaunt's. I first got down to Footscray in November of the 1978/79 season. We were back living in Werribee, and Dad took me down and we met Lindsay James, the captain/coach; Ken Eastwood, who was a selector and captaining the 2nds; Jim Mann, the president; and Ron Gaunt, who was the bowling coach. Ron asked me what I did. I told him I bat and bowl a bit. Typical talkative and informative seventeen year old. They were all standing there, trying to work out if I could ever make a cricketer at Footscray. They asked me to have a bowl so I went into the senior net and after three balls, Ron said, 'Right son, you don't bat anymore, you're a bowler.' Happy days! I like being told what to do.

Ron played three Tests over seven years. He was flown in as a replacement for one Test against South Africa in 1958.

He was an Ashes tourist in 1961 but only played one Test despite taking 40 first-class wickets on the tour. He wasn't afraid to put it in short. My favourite sort of fast bowler!

I had just turned 17 when I started at Footscray, and every night that I trained, Ron stood at the top of the mark and worked with me. Every delivery he would make a comment, or encourage me or suggest I could try something subtle to improve my bowling. Every night for three years. As much as anyone he turned me into the bowler I became. He emphasised the idea of training hard and I will never forget one time when he said to me, 'The harder you work in the easy times, the easier it becomes in the hard times.' What that meant to me was, the harder I worked at training and the more I put into training, the more I was going to get back in a game. A former Test player who gave up so much of his time to try to get me to be the best that I could be. Legend.

Ken Eastwood

Tests
1 (1971), 5 runs (5), 1 wicket

First Class
42 (1959–1972), 2722 runs (221), 6 wickets (1 for 10), 27 catches

Ken Eastwood made his Test debut in an Ashes Test under Ian Chappell, opening the batting with Keith Stackpole. Ken was aged 35. He also bowled five overs of left-arm chinaman and took a wicket. I've always said that you should respect those that have done better than you and he has a better bowling average than me in Test cricket so I love him.

I got to know Ken Eastwood when I got down to Footscray. I played my first game in the 3rds then moved up to the 2nds, and Ken Eastwood was captain. I was seventeen and he seemed ancient. I was born on the same date as him, but 26 years later.

You learn so much from your leaders and Ken Eastwood was a great leader. His leadership came from his strong, clear mindset. It was black and white, no grey areas. Perhaps I just like simple instructions because I can understand them, but he always seemed very direct and very specific when he was telling me my role in the team.

He had some military background and it showed in how he went about things. On the ground he was really hard at it, and off the ground, he was still intensely passionate about cricket as a sport but could back away from any particular match. For a young bloke playing in the 2nds, to have a guy of his calibre captaining the side was a really steep learning curve for me. We won the 2nds premiership in my first year at the club.

Ken still gets down to Footscray–Edgewater for games. I have always enjoyed the company of those blokes who just undeniably love the game and Kenny Eastwood is one of those blokes.

Lindsay James

The greatest man God ever put breath into. Captain of the side when I won my first senior premiership. Enough said. Lindsay James was one of the toughest blokes that I ever played cricket with. He was a hard nut and he expected everyone to play the same way. His philosophy on cricket was, We may not be the best team but if we are the best-prepared team then we've got a chance. He was the stereotypical wicket-keeper: short, nuggetty and tough as nails. He expected everyone to be committed to doing their best. If you were having a good day or a bad day it didn't matter, as long as you gave it everything.

He used to train us hard and the thing that I loved about him as a leader was that he wouldn't ask the players to do anything he wouldn't do himself. If we were being punished for a poor performance or getting fitness driven into us, he was always there doing it. We were all in it together and he led from the front.

Halfway through my second year at Footscray I got into the senior side, playing with men like Lindsay and Viddy Richardson who made a lot of runs, as did Barry

Watson. Senior blokes who really taught me a lot about how to play the game. Be fierce and uncompromising on the ground, and what happens on the ground stays on the ground.

An example of Lindsay's leadership and management of players was the grand final of the 1979/80 season—my second year at the club and my first in the seniors. There had been a bit of rain around so there were a few rain delays but we got 221 on the board. For a three-day grand final it wasn't a great score and the experts were telling us that it was a bit skinny and we wouldn't win. We were playing St Kilda and we had them six for 80 overnight. Geoff Tamblyn, now the chairman of Cricket Victoria, and John Emburey, the English off spinner, were batting. Two very experienced players with all day to make 150. We were on top but in cricket, you can't assume anything.

The umpires came in and gave us the five-minute call before play. I will always remember that moment. First year in the seniors, a district cricket grand final, I was pretty nervous. As a young bloke and as a fast bowler, you want to know exactly what's expected of you. Before we walked out of the rooms, Lindsay came over to me. 'Right Merv, you're starting.'

'Okay,' I replied, hoping there was going to be more but not wanting to ask. I shouldn't have worried.

'If you bowl one delivery in the batsman's half of the pitch you will never play cricket for Footscray again.'

Now that's black and white. That's clear. I knew what was expected of me. So I spent all day bouncing the crap out of them. I didn't take any wickets but I handed out a few bruises and we rolled them for 120. Happy days!

Viddy Richardson

Another bloke who should have played state cricket. When I got down to Footscray, Viddy was entrenched in the senior team and in my first couple of years there he was the number one player at Footscray. He batted number three and wasn't unsettled by pace. He played the cross-batted shots pretty well, particularly to the leg side. He was a thoughtful batsman with a solid defence and worked the ball down the ground early in his innings. He was a great player for Footscray for a very long time and was unlucky not to play for Victoria. He was in the state squad for a while but for some reason didn't get a run in the Victorian side and I don't know why.

Our home ground, the Western Oval, was a very green deck and the grass tended to be kept a bit longer than other cricket grounds because we shared the ground with the Footscray Football Club. It wasn't a batsman-friendly place and visiting bowlers used to get a bit excited about the bounce in the wicket. But Viddy used to make his 750–800 runs year on year. There wasn't a lot of incentive to hit the ball along the ground in front of the wicket so Viddy got a lot of value square of the wicket on the leg side. He became an excellent player of the short ball because hitting it square and in the air was the best way to make runs there. How many balls we saw sail over the Doug Hawkins wing onto Gordon Street!

Of course, being a stalwart of the team and an experienced player, Viddy took me under his wing when I started my senior stint and showed me the ropes. One of the ways he looked after me was that he was very careful to manage my workload. We hear a lot these days about fast bowlers' playing load and training load, but in the late seventies Viddy was ahead of his time. At the Western Oval our practice nets backed into the grandstand and if you played the hook shot it usually went up into the stand. Viddy was very good on the hook and he got it a bit squarer so it actually used to go out to the car park at the Barkly Street end of the ground. On really hot nights when I was feeling a little bit fatigued I used to throw in the bouncers so he could hook me and if he got it right, I'd have ten minutes off going to get the ball. Then I would give him another one and the next one would take me fifteen minutes to find. That's still the best workload-management strategy I've come across!

He was also responsible for another very important part of my education: he showed me how a district cricketer should play up after a game. It's debatable whether that was a good or bad thing but I had a very good time!

Michael Haysman

First class

103 (1982–1994), 5977 runs (180), 5 wickets (2 for 19), 140 catches

Michael Haysman was a very, very good player for South Australia. I first met him when he played against Victoria at the Junction Oval in 1982/83. It was Mike's first year in the South Aussie team. He and David Hookes came together at four for 48. Rick Darling, Wayne Phillips, Andrew Hilditch and John Inverarity were out, so we were well into the tail when the young bloke came in to bat. Mike made 153 and Hookesy made 193!

He struck me immediately as a talented batsman. Tall. Stood upright and had all the shots. Showed me the full face of the bat down the ground. He also had the ability to pull the ball and seemed to have a lot of time if you bowled short to him, so there was really no way that I found to pressure him.

Later that summer, he and I, with Greg Matthews and Robbie Kerr, were selected to receive Esso scholarships. They paid for us to play a year of 2nd XI county cricket. So we spent an Aussie winter not playing footy, and that year learning more about the game of cricket and the English conditions.

I was at Essex and he was at Leicestershire, but I got to know him pretty well through the Esso program. I knew he was a very good cricketer and I found out he is a great bloke to go with it. I hoped we might one day play together for Australia, but he went on the rebel tour to South Africa in 1985/86 and 1986/87 and did pretty well in the second year. He ended up moving to South Africa, and playing at Transvaal and Northern Transvaal. He had a twelve-year first-class career, then become a commentator and is now the face of televised cricket in South Africa. Mike's story shows what cricket can do for you. He played in Youth Tests for Australia and started his first-class career by averaging 57 in his first Sheffield Shield season. Then he had to choose between a rebel tour and a possible Test career and took a path that had an enormously positive influence on his life. Must have been scared of the possibility of having to room with me!

Michael O'Keefe

Tocker! Michael O'Keefe was a Warrnambool boy who came to Footscray in the mid-eighties and played there for many years. He made a mountain of runs at Footscray and is one of those players who could have made it at state level. One year he had a trial match against a Victorian country XI. A few of his Footscray teammates and I made the trip down to Sale to watch him play. Unfortunately, he had no luck on that day and wasn't given another chance. That's one of the cruel things about cricket. Most batsmen will consider a century a successful innings, but anything less than a hundred is not. Yet only the very best cricketers in the history of the game average more than 50. So at least twice out of every three innings, history says a batsman will fail. That is one of the reasons cricket is such a test of character. Tocker, who I know would have acquitted himself very well at first-class level, only ever got one chance. The way he played the game at Footscray is testament to the quality of the man.

I was in the state team and on the fringes of the Test team when I met him, and he impressed me from the start. He was an exceptional person, an outstanding player, a great leader and a rock-solid teammate. He was a very hard trainer and as competitive a cricketer as I've seen. And like any champion, the tougher it got on the ground the better he was. He was pretty much like that off the ground too. The tougher the celebrations got, the more Tocker thrived! He was the ultimate cricketer who got the best out of himself and made his teammates do the same because no one wanted to let Tocker down.

Rainer Reber

Rainer Reber should have played Test cricket for no other reason than that he is a great bloke. He played in the Victorian Under-19s team against Pakistan and he played in the Victorian 2nd XI. In my 21 years of senior cricket at Footscray I only ever played with two wicket-keepers: Lindsay James and Rainer Reber. Rainer has gloved more of my deliveries than any other player at any level of the game.

Rainer is a legend to me because I played with him for so long. I went to school with him. Played with him at Werribee before we went to Footscray—although he has probably erased those memories. We weren't all that kind to Rainer at school. The word 'bullying' comes to mind, and I'm not proud of myself. But he was three years younger than me and my good mate Snapper Whiting. Snapper was also a wicket-keeper at Werribee. We had this young bloke coming through and sort of nipping at our heels so he had to be put in his place, didn't he? So I'm surprised that Rainer even talks to me.

But mate, I love him to death. He is one of my favourite people to go out and have a beer with. Absolutely fantastic to sit down, have a coffee and talk serious cricket talk with because he has a wealth of knowledge about the game.

I've always said that, in a cricket environment, my best two mates in a team are the wicket-keeper, number one, and the physiotherapist, number two. I had a lot to do with all the wicket-keepers that I played with because basically they know how hard you're hitting the gloves and they know what the wicket is doing in comparison to other bowlers. Ian Healy was great to play with and a great mate, and so were Michael Dimattina and Darren Berry—and with Ray it was no different.

Quite often Rainer is not taken seriously by those who know him well, because at times he has his own logic. But gee, he is just a good bloke to have around and a good bloke in the trenches. As a teammate you knew that you were going to get the very best out of him, every game. He may not make a run but he wouldn't throw his wicket away. If you played with him, you loved him, although I dare say if you played against him you'd be scratching your head thinking, What the hell is going on here? He would have been an absolute pain in the arse to play against.

But he was enthusiastic about everything that he did: cricket, wicket-keeping, coaching soccer. And drinking. Not very good at it but very enthusiastic, and that's what you've got to love about the bloke. If you're going to commit to something, don't do it half-arsed.

He holds the record for the most senior games played at Footscray. So he played a lot of games. I think he's got most dismissals along with that and I suppose if you're worth your salt and have played the most games as a wicket-keeper you should have the most dismissals. His problem was that he didn't make many runs, so he wasn't seen to be the greatest of batsman and he used to bat at number eleven. Most coaches start calling the batting order from the openers and go down the list. I reckon our captains at Footscray used to say, 'Rainer, you're eleven' and then do the rest of the line-up.

But the thing about him was, he just kept getting not outs. I think he still holds the record for the most not outs by a batsman in Premier Cricket in Victoria. It was amazing how many times we would be nine down with twenty runs to get and we'd get across the line. His argument was that if he kept getting not outs, shouldn't he bat higher? I thought it was a very sound argument.

Rainer Reber: all of the things that make cricket the great game that it is. It doesn't matter what level you play, if you get the best out of yourself when the pressure is on, you are a champion.

Ian Callen

Tests
1 (1978), 26 runs (22 not out), 6 wickets (3 for 83), 1 catch

ODIs
5 (1978–1982), 6 runs (3 not out), 5 wickets (3 for 24), 2 catches

When I first got into the Victorian team 'Mad Dog' was the senior bowler. He took me under his wing and taught me a lot about touring life, and possibly not all of it was positive! But it was all useful. Callen was a touch over 6 foot tall but had a magnificent action. It was slick. Fluent. I remember sitting at training when I first got into the state squad and watching him bowl and thinking, How good is this bloke! He generated great pace but was at a disadvantage because of his lack of height. He played his Test match the season after making his first-class debut, so others had seen his promise too. He struggled with back injuries from then on but played the occasional One Day International.

The greatest thing that Ian taught me (apart from touring skills) was the difference between the different levels of cricket. He pointed out that at all levels of cricket you do three things: bat, bowl and field. When you're bowling in club cricket, you might bowl a bad ball an over and get away with it. In state cricket you might bowl a bad ball every second or third over and get away with it. At Test level, because the wickets are so much truer and the batsmen are so much better, every bad ball you bowl gets dealt with. If a Test batsman wants to hit a bad ball for four, he will. So basically what he was saying was that the higher you go, the margin for error gets narrower. He used to instil that in me when we were training: You need to improve if you're going to step up the ladder and play a higher level of cricket.

It made me concentrate on the quality of training. Mad Dog taught me that I needed to concentrate on eliminating bad balls even in the nets. This is something Bob Simpson echoed when I first got into the Australian side too: it is the quality of training that makes you better, not the quantity. If you bowl for two hours, you can't maintain your maximum intensity over two hours. But if you are bowling for 45 minutes and you're doing everything spot on, that's going to lead to more improvement. That to me was a very important lesson.

He had a truly thoughtful approach to getting the best out of himself as a cricketer, but he was called Mad Dog because he was. Another important thing he taught me was how to dose my effort. Being new to the four-day game when I joined the Victorian team, Ian got me to understand that if you could keep from bowling bad balls, you didn't need to go flat out the whole match. There were periods when you did, such as with a new ball or when you needed a breakthrough, but he showed me that sometimes you just need to be patient, bowl accurately, build pressure and wait. Let the game come to you. This was also one of the important touring skills he passed on to me. He showed me that in a crowded pub, you should make a big effort to push through the crowd to get to the bar, but it was critical to make the most of that effort by getting to the bar beside the taps. Then you could just wait. Let the barman come to you. Legend.

Rod McCurdy

First Class

86 (1979–1993), 725 runs (55), 305 wickets (7 for 55), 25 catches

ODIs

11 (1985), 33 runs (13 not out), 12 wickets (3 for 19), 1 catch

Rod McCurdy, or Pup as he is affectionately known, was in the Victorian state side when I was first selected. He took 38 wickets for the season of 1982/83 and was a great example for a young bowler coming into the Victorian side. Whether it was the first over of the first day or the last over of the last day, his effort didn't waver. He would be constantly testing the batsmen, always at good pace. He was also fantastic in the field and awesome with the bat. He always took them on. He loved his role as an unpredictable lower-order batsman and whether it was hooking or cutting or back foot driving, he'd just hit the ball hard. When I think about how I played the game, it is clear there was a lot about Pup's approach that influenced me.

He played a few one dayers for Australia and would have been a chance for Test selection but went on the rebel tour of South Africa in 1985 and that was the end of his international career. After the rebels were forgiven, he played for Tasmania and South Australia as well as county cricket for Derbyshire, and then for three South African provinces.

A man who loved his cricket and loved a contest.

James Brayshaw

First Class

75 (1987–1997), 4934 runs (146), 10 wickets (2 for 15), 43 catches

The Three Jamies: James Brayshaw, Jamie Cox and Jamie Siddons. In my time playing cricket they were the three unluckiest blokes not to play Test cricket. You can only pick eleven, but these three guys were unlucky.

James Brayshaw gets a hard time from his colleagues on Victoria's *Footy Show* for not having played at the top level. If you look at his Sheffield Shield figures he has a record that would have got him into the Test team in another era: an opening batsman for ten years with an average of 45 in the toughest first-class competition in the world. He made his first-class debut at twenty, and the Test line-up in the late eighties was one of the best in a generation. If he had been a little bit earlier or a little bit later he would have been picked and would have acquitted himself very well.

He didn't like to be called Jamie or Jim, it was always James. 'G'day Jimbo,' always got the response, 'The name is James.' I'm going to be honest: this, along with the way that he pranced around on the field, made me take an instant dislike to him. So whenever I played against him I would give him everything all day, because that was usually how long it took me to get him out. But I always had enormous respect for him. He was good enough to get the very best out of me every time I played him, and more often than not he came out on top. One day at the MCG he played and missed. 'Oh for Christ's sake, Brayshaw, you haven't improved in ten years!'

Jimbo looked over and said, 'Listen Merv, I've had enough of this crap. You've been giving it to me for ten years. Just shut up and bowl!'

'Oh okay.'

We sat down and had a beer after that day's play and reminisced over all the sledging I'd given him and all the grief he had given me and decided to call a truce. And I decided he was a much better bloke with a beer in his hand than a bat.

I admire him because he loved it tough. His performances against Victoria for a long time were outstanding. He was one of the most courageous players I played against.

Jamie Cox

First Class

264 (1987–2005), 18,614 runs (250), 5 wickets (3 for 46), 124 catches

Jamie Cox batted high in the order. Early in his career he batted at four or five and then went up to open. Unlucky not to play Test cricket but would have had to displace the likes of Mark Taylor, Geoff Marsh, Michael Slater and Matthew Hayden, so you can understand why he didn't play. But someone who makes 18,000 first-class runs without playing Test cricket is pretty rare.

He was very like Greg Chappell in the way that he batted. Upright, very correct, in behind the line, showed the full face of the bat. You couldn't hustle him for pace at all and he played all around the wicket. I used to try to ruffle his feathers a bit verbally but nothing I said ever seemed to worry him too much. He went about his business and was a good player for a long time. I would have loved to have played alongside him.

Jamie Siddons

ODIs

1 (1988), 32 runs

First Class

160 (1984–2000), 11,587 runs (245), 2 wickets (1 for 8), 206 catches

When Victoria started to rebuild in the early eighties, we had three senior players: Dav Whatmore, Paul Hibbert and Ray Bright. And then we had a heap of young blokes, including Michael Dimattina, Tony Dodemaide and Simon O'Donnell.

When Jamie Siddons came in he was just extraordinary. He became one of the best friends I made through cricket. I used to love watching him play, because whereas most blokes trying to score quickly go leg side he had a great ability to hit the ball over cover and mid-off. It was a skill he'd developed playing juniors at Robinvale, where they only had a net on the leg side, so if he hit the ball to leg it went into the nets, and he couldn't see how far he'd hit it. So they used to have these competitions to see who could hit the ball furthest over the other side. That became his strength.

I always had huge respect for Jamie. In 1987/88 on a flight to Perth for a Shield game, he took it on himself to fire me up. He suggested I was taking it easy on my Australian teammates and he didn't think Victorian cricket was as important to me as it had been in the past. I was pretty angry. Even after the airline people took the straitjacket off me and told me they weren't going to press charges I was still cranky. I think it was a good thing that we had to bat first so I had a few days to cool down. As it was, I split one of the West Australian opener's eyebrows, broke Graeme Wood's hand and parted Kim Hughes' hair before getting him out lbw for seven. Great people skills had Jamie.

He was also the best fieldsman that I ever played with. Head and shoulders above anyone else. He has hands the size of baseball mitts. In the slips he would take the piss. Dead set. Dodders told me he used to be terrified to go into the slips on the last day of a Shield match because Jamie would instigate this game where you had to close your eyes until the ball had hit the bat. So from halfway through the bowler's run-up you had to have the nerve to keep your eyes shut! Who could do that? Jamie was just fearless.

Gary Cosier

Tests
18 (1975–1978), 897 runs (168), 5 wickets (2 for 26), 14 catches

ODIs
9 (1975–1979), 154 runs (84), 14 wickets (5 for 18), 4 catches

Gary Cosier got into the Test team just before the World Series Cricket days. He had forearms like fence posts and although he had red hair, I just loved the way that he batted. With his short, short back lift, he wasn't hurried by bowlers. He played both off the back foot and front foot and with punchy drives that had as much power as anyone else who played the game.

He started his first-class career at Victoria, where the top six in the order when everyone was available contained Keith Stackpole, Bill Lawry, Ian Redpath, Paul Sheahan and John Scholes, so getting a spot wasn't straightforward. He made a century in his first Test innings, against the West Indies, and played in the Centenary Test in 1977. He stuck with the national team when the World Series split happened, and played under Bob Simpson and Graham Yallop.

Soon after he made the Australian side, I went to play district cricket at Footscray. I enjoyed watching Gary's career. He went to play for Queensland and then South Australia, but found his way back to Victoria. He played district cricket for St Kilda when he returned so I had the opportunity to play against him. He ended up playing a lot of club cricket so I got to know him on and off the ground. Isn't it great when someone you admire for their excellence turns out to be everything that you imagined them to be? He was a tough competitor who didn't take a backward step and a real good bloke off the ground.

The St Kilda blokes were renowned for just taking the piss out of each other. In one of the games we played against them at the Western Oval, St Kilda were fielding and Warren Whiteside picked the ball up and had a shot at the stumps for a run out. It missed the stumps and went for four overthrows. As the bowler was halfway through his run-up for the next ball, Cosier stopped the bowler and took the third slip out and put it over to square leg. The wicket-keeper piped up (as they always do) and asked, 'What are you doing that for?'

'Saving overthrows,' came back from Gary, quick as a flash.

Another day against St Kilda on a green pitch at the Western Oval, I was running in and bowling leg spinners at Warren Whiteside because he was one of my mates so I was trying to look after him. Of course I was trying to kill Cosier when I bowled to him because he was such a tough competitor. Cosier said to me, 'Oh that's alright, look after your little fat mate down the other end and bowl slower balls to him and try and kill me, you prick!' Having a crack at me and at his teammate all in one sledge. Funny day.

I wouldn't say that Gary Cosier was over-endowed with supreme talent but he got the most out of himself through his competitive nature and his character. And he always had a good sense of humour. I suppose you grow that with red hair.

Peter Bedford

First Class

39 (1966–1973), 1602 runs (134 not out), 45 wickets (5 for 40), 40 catches

Peter Bedford, Brownlow medallist. Awarded to the fairest and best player in the nation's premier Australian Rules competition. I can't remember too much of Peter Bedford playing either cricket or football. I just know that he played for South Melbourne and he won a Brownlow medal. He played state cricket for Victoria. I've had more to do with him through Crusaders Cricket, which is a coaching development group who go out and play against schools on Wednesday afternoons. I've got to know Peter over the last ten years and his tenacity and his passion for the game is unbelievable.

He'd be more than ten years older than me but to see him run around the field, you'd never believe it. If someone whacks a ball to him he will jump in front of it and get his shins in the way of it. It comes off his shins and he'll just throw it back and walk off. If I get hit in the shins I'm hobbling for about a week.

I remember one game, where he was standing at first slip and I was at second slip, hoping that the ball didn't come my way. At one point, a nicked ball looks like it's going to hit my left foot, so being the courageous cricketer I am I get my foot out of the road and turn my back on the ball, which you're not supposed to do at second slip. Peter dives across and takes a catch. Doesn't know what the problem is. Sixty years old and he is doing that.

Another day we're playing on a slow, slow wicket. Two of our batsmen are trying to push the run rate along by cutting the ball between the fieldsmen at forward point and backward point but it's not working. Peter is sitting there getting more and more frustrated. 'These blokes are trying to hit the ball too hard. All they've got to do is place it and they get two runs every time, but they're trying to hit the boundary and they're picking out one of the fieldsmen every time. They need to be more patient.' I think to myself, That's easy to say from here.

A wicket falls and he gets out there, gets himself going and starts playing gentle cut shots between the two players. Again and again, cut shot between the two players, two runs. No macho hard hitting, just timing and finesse. I am still amazed at how different blokes think about the game. I reckon he was just doing it to show the kids you don't have to hit boundaries to hit runs.

Having seen his approach at his age, I can tell he would have been a tough nut to play cricket against, and it's easy to see why he was one of the best footballers of his generation. Having the opportunity to get to know him and see the passion he has for the game is inspiring. He's up there for me.

Ian Wrigglesworth

First class

6 (1993–2000), 353 runs (85), 9 wickets (3 for 72), 7 catches

Ian Wrigglesworth is a great man and is as passionate about cricket as anyone I have met. We were in the state squad together for a number of years and if not for Simon O'Donnell and Tony Dodemaide, Ian would have played 100 Sheffield Shield matches for Victoria. He was a journeyman of district cricket for a long time. He played at five different clubs because he was a much sought-after cricketer. He was an honest, tough cricketer who could hold his own at club cricket level as either a batsman or a bowler. He could bat in the top six and open the bowling and often bowled many overs in the day. Unfortunately for him, at the peak of his game, another fine Victorian, Tony Dodemaide, was playing 184 first-class matches as an all-rounder, so Wriggles rarely got a look in.

He is another country boy who is still playing at Sale and I talk to him a lot about the state of the game. He is passionate about how cricket should be developed in primary schools. He says cricket is a unique game that to the uninitiated needs a long time to be played. He has been advocating for years that state players should be going into primary schools and getting short games being played so everyone can have a crack. The Twenty20 format is the perfect vehicle for teaching the game at school level and Wriggles has been talking about it for twenty years. Prophet and legend.

John Scholes

First Class

62 (1968–1982), 3201 runs (156), 1 wicket (1 for 28), 44 catches

Johnny Scholes was a champion. I wouldn't say he was the most naturally talented cricketer I knew, but certainly one of the most courageous and determined.

I first ran into 'Barrel' when I was working at the sports store at Werribee. He was a sales rep for one of the batting companies and he used to come in and give us a hard time. I knew who he was because the ABC used to telecast the last session of the Shield matches on TV. The other reason I knew who he was is probably the same reason I was working in the sports store rather than being at school. On a Friday during the cricket season, I would go to school until lunchtime, then catch a train to the MCG and watch the state games. If I didn't do that, I would go home and watch the last session on TV after school from four to six so I knew who all the state players were!

Johnny Scholes was the captain of the state side when I got in. Usually when I was put into a new team I would feel a little bit intimidated by the captain. But Scholesy gave me a hard time right from the start and I felt very comfortable with that. Strong opponents made him raise the level of his own game. He had some wonderful battles on green wickets at the WACA, when we would watch him in awe of his courage and his ability.

He had a great perspective on the game and thought about cricket at a team tactics level. Scholesy was a positive bloke who kept the game moving so if he was captain or in charge he wanted to give as much opportunity for a result as he could. I learnt that at Footscray under Lindsay James and certainly in the Victorian side under him and at the time, couldn't understand why other teams didn't always play that way.

But the other thing that Barrel taught me was that not everyone plays cricket the same way, and as a player you have to accept how your opponent plays. Not every team is always looking for a result. Some teams are there to be competitive, some are there to just make it hard for the opposition to win. Although it has always been in my nature to be looking for a win, he taught me that I needed to accept that in some circumstances a draw is a legitimate result that is often not easy to achieve. In his view, that is part of the greatness of the game.

He went on to coach Victoria and turned the Victorian side around and created a great environment to play in. Then he finished my first-class career by dropping me from the Victorian squad. He wanted me to retire gracefully, but that isn't a word I understand. Just look at my run-up. Barrel gave me every possible chance leading up to the 1996/97 season, but I wasn't making the grade with my fitness. I should have known something was up when he invited me to a press conference at Cricket Victoria and he walked in carrying a knife. He knew I didn't want to retire, but he had the courage to look me in the eye and tell me I was gone. What more could you ask for?

Warren Whiteside

First Class

21 (1983–1988), 908 runs (111), 13 wickets (2 for 6), 12 catches

Warren was probably one of the most naturally gifted cricketers that I played with. Unfortunately he played at a time where talent wasn't enough to get to the top.

He won three Ryder Medals, awarded for the best player in district cricket in Victoria. Cricket Victoria are very good about looking after the guys who have won Ryder Medals, and they used to send out a pass for every day of cricket at the MCG to medallists. Warren wrote to the Cricket Victoria CEO, Ken Jacobs, pointing out that as he had won three medals, he should be getting three tickets so he could bring his mates to MCG games!

He's a quirky, funny bloke. There was a game in Adelaide when we bowled South Australia out. We've gone in to bat and we're quickly three for not many. Warren has to go in just before lunch to face a single over. He nicks the first ball through slip for four. Nicks the second ball through slip for another four. He comes off at lunch and says, 'I'm the top scorer in the top five, surely I get a game next week?' He was happy with that.

He was a really competitive bloke who did a lot on natural talent and competitiveness but was another player who played cricket a generation too late and probably didn't fit in with the changing nature of professional cricket. He was never going to give himself an ulcer worrying about his body fat—but gee he had a great sense of humour!

Colin Miller

Tests

18 (1998–2001), 174 runs (43), 69 wickets (5 for 32), 6 catches

First Class

126 (1985–2002), 1533 runs (62), 446 wickets (7 for 49), 39 catches

Funky Col Medina. Everyone will remember the Col Miller that played cricket for Australia. Got picked as a 34-year-old off spin bowler, slogged the ball around a bit. We had him at Footscray as a young bloke and he has not changed one iota. Still just a loose cannon. Loves his Scotch and Coke. The one thing that did change was that when he was at Footscray, he was a fast–medium swing bowler who slogged the ball around a bit. The chameleon Colin Miller transformed himself into whatever was needed. And not just the colour of his hair.

He played a couple of games for Victoria. Went to South Australia and did okay there. Then he went to Tasmania and all of a sudden he is this bloke who was almost opening the bowling with his medium pace, and then would bowl off spin when the ball had got old. He was a creative character.

I can remember him at Footscray in his early twenties talking about being a switch hitter—going out and facing up as a right hander and as the bowler was running in, changing to left handed to upset the field. Everyone would look at him with a fair bit of dubiosity and yet that's what is happening in the game today. We see it in Twenty20 and the modern game, and everyone is taken aback when it happens and remarking what a fantastic initiative it is. Colin Miller was thinking about this stuff 25 years ago. Flexibility, adaptability, usefulness to the team—that's what he was all about.

His thoughts on the game were always interesting. His contribution to cricket was fantastic. The thing that really amazed me about him was that in March 2001 he won the Australian Test Player of the Year for the 2000/01 season, in what was the best Test team in the world, then played in one match of a three-Test series in India that same month, and never played Test cricket again.

Colin was a thinking larrikin's cricketer. He spent time wondering how to have an impact on how the game was played, before the game knew it needed changing. He was a bloke before his time. He was a good cricketer and a very solid teammate. He was also one of the blokes you wanted to be around after the match!

Alan Davidson

Tests

44 (1953–1963), 1328 runs (80), 186 wickets (7 for 93), 42 catches

The best way to get an insightful perspective on the game is to talk to blokes who have been around it for a long time and have played at the highest level. One of the great qualities of cricket is the way that its fundamentals don't change. It is a number of one-on-one confrontations between batsman and bowler, where the bowler needs to use every resource he has to force an error from the batsman. The batsman has to resist the bowler, protect his wicket, but in most cases needs to take risks to score runs. The winner is the one who tips the balance in their own favour. There are many resources available and there are factors that can't be controlled that will influence the outcome. Learning the skills of bowling takes time and learning how to best use the resources can take a lifetime.

Alan Davidson played for New South Wales and Australia for a long time as a bustling left hander, and hard-hitting late-order batsman. I always admired Gary Gilmour and to me, Alan Davidson played a very similar role to him—although Davidson was a little bit better with the bat than Gilmour and a lot better with the ball. Davo batted between six and nine for Australia, which made him an outstanding player. He could open the bowling with his left armers so he was a real all-rounder. When you talk about all-rounders in the game these days it's a bloke who can possibly hold down number eight—like a Mitch Johnson, who is a bowler that can bat. But Davo was a genuine bowler and a genuine batsman.

I remember when I met Alan. I was playing for Victoria against Tasmania, which means I was trying to dismiss David Boon. This was in the first couple of years of my time in the Victorian team. I thought that I needed to go at Boonie hard to get him out but Boonie, who has always been very good on the back foot, got some runs and we ended up losing the game. We came off the ground and Alan Davidson was down in our rooms. At that stage, I didn't know who he was. He had probably been introduced to the team but it hadn't registered with me.

I'm sitting there, worn out, and pissed off that we had lost and that Boonie had scored some runs off my bowling. Davidson comes over and sits down and starts talking about the game and the pitch, then he starts asking me questions.

'What were you trying to do?'

'I was trying to take a wicket.'

'But how were you trying to take it?'

'Well, we had to get a wicket.'

'But how?'

'Well, run in and bowl fast.'

He told me that bowling on that wicket was like trying to get blood from a stone. There was no life in the wicket so you had to think about the way you went about it. At the time I was thinking, Who is this old fart? But the longer we spoke about it, the more I saw it made sense. What I'd done is gone out there and thought, Right, I've just got to get a wicket. Got to bowl as fast as I can to get a wicket. Boonie was a good player who didn't have too much trouble with pace so I wasn't putting him under pressure. Bull-at-a-gate stuff can work if conditions are in your favour, but sometimes you've got to take a backward step and say, Let's prevent scoring and build up pressure that way.

I went away from that conversation thinking, Well that's a lesson learnt, isn't it? One conversation with Alan Davidson that went for maybe half an hour, and I had changed my approach to bowling for ever.

PART

4

THE REST OF THE WORLD

Cricket's a funny game. Fancy ending up enjoying watching the play of so many blokes you tried to kill with a cricket ball! That is why we love the game. It lets us make heroes of our team and villains of the opposition, but we all know, as players and as fans, that we secretly admire the best of the other side.

All these blokes were unfortunate enough to not be Australian, but I would have loved to have had them as teammates.

Derek Pringle

Tests
30 (1982–1992), 695 runs (63), 70 wickets (5 for 95), 10 catches

ODIs
44 (1982–1993), 425 runs (49 not out), 44 wickets (4 for 42), 11 catches

I first came across Derek Pringle at Essex. I went there on an Esso scholarship to play for the Essex County 2nd XI. He was playing international cricket at that time and he came back to Essex between Tests. He would have a couple of games in the 2nds if the 1sts weren't playing and he wanted top-up games or was coming back from injury. I played a few with Derek, and he is probably one of the smartest cricketers I've ever met. He is well educated, well spoken, and very methodical in his approach to life. These are qualities you don't often find in cricketers, and certainly not all three in the one cricketer!

He was a solid performer for England over time, and a very solid performer for Essex. His best wasn't outstanding but his worst was never too bad. His best was five for 95 in Tests and he got a couple of first-class centuries. Being 6 foot 4 helps in a pace bowler, but it'd be selling him short to think his achievements were due to his height. He batted at number seven and he would get good runs for you too. He was a genuine all-rounder at first-class level.

Because I met him in 1983 at Essex, I followed his career and we crossed paths in a few Test matches. We still cross paths now as he is a journalist working for the English media. He has not changed in that time. He has a very dry, cynical and sarcastic view of life and I've got to say they are three traits I really love in a person. He is also very thought provoking with the articles that he writes. He has the insight of one who has been inside the sheds, and he writes about what he thinks is going on behind the scenes and about his view on the game. This takes a lot of courage to write because if it backfires he is going to cop a bit of grief.

Apart from being a journalist, the other thing that pissed me off about Derek was that I couldn't sledge him. He's too smart. No matter what I said, Derek would just smile at me, and say, 'Oh come on Merv, don't be like that.' Too smart to even return fire. He gave me nothing and made me smile, so I was worse off than when I started. I always got told, Don't sledge anyone smarter than yourself because it's going to come back to haunt you, and that is good advice. But knowing each other like we did, it took away that mystique so I'd give it a go with Derek anyway. After all, if I didn't sledge anyone who was smarter than me, I wouldn't have the opportunity to sledge too many people, would I?

David Gower

Tests

117 (1978–1992), 8231 runs (215), 1 wicket (1 for 1), 74 catches

ODIs

114 (1978–1991), 3170 runs (158), 44 catches

Watching David Gower bat was like watching a barmaid pour your first beer on a hot day: beautiful to watch but it seems to happen in slow motion. He copped a lot of criticism when he got out, very similar to Mark Waugh in many ways, because he looked so lazy and disinterested at times. Disinterested, not uninterested. Sometimes I think he had so much time that as the ball approached him, he considered three or four options and then played the most difficult shot just to see if he could do it, regardless of the risks. But when he was batting well he just looked so elegant and in control. I grew up watching him playing against Australia in the 1981 and 1985 Ashes tours to England.

In 1989 we were going to Arundel to play the Duchess of Norfolk's XI in the first tour game and A.B. said, 'I don't care who else gets runs, David Gower doesn't get runs.'

That approach was something that A.B. took from the great West Indian sides. You target the opposition captain and you target the tail. If you can break both of those you go a long way to winning the game. In 1989, David Gower had a price on his head.

For so long, Border said, games between England and Australia had almost seemed like charity matches. The English side would just come out, and be very comfortable, and we had to remove that comfort zone. With Gower, and Mike Gatting and Graham Gooch, whether you spoke to them or not wasn't up to you. Verballing them was not an option because you didn't want to get into a battle with them. It would fire them up and they would get themselves into the game. And we weren't to chat to them either. Neutral, anti-social silence.

David Gower was a beautiful batsman to watch. When he got going, there was none better. The shots that he played, his cover drive, his cutting, his pulling, the flicks down the leg side, things like that, just made you think, He is just a great player.

The flick down the leg side was one of Gower's strengths that we made into a weakness. At team meetings we sit down and talk about the strengths and weaknesses of every player. We even examine their fielding. Are they quick to the ball? Do they have strong arms? In the team meeting before the First Test match at Headingley in 1989, we were talking about strengths and weaknesses of batsmen. Allan Border threw it open and asked if anyone had any ideas about David Gower. Geoff Lawson came up with the David Gower leg slip. Everyone looked at Geoff and thought, Mate, you don't bowl leg stump to a player like that.

Well, Geoff Lawson got him out the first three times he batted in the series. Just flicking down leg side. We had him caught. Instead of having a fine leg we would have almost a leg slipper and a bloke just behind square, and he had to adjust his game. It paid dividends. It wasn't every ball but just the occasional one thrown down the leg side and Geoff Lawson was very good because he had the right shape. That's the difference between strategy and tactics. A.B. had the strategy, Geoff Lawson suggested the tactic. It worked.

Gower was England captain in 32 matches between 1982 and the end of the 1989 Ashes. During that series he was controlling a team that contained four former Test captains: Botham, Gooch, Gatting and Emburey. During a difficult time for English cricket and many changes of leadership, his approach to batting was seen in a far worse light than if he had been playing for a successful side. But anyone who scores more than 8000 Test runs is committed to his performance and has more ability and more mental toughness than most. Legend.

Robin Smith

Tests
62 (1988–1996), 4236 runs (175), 39 catches

ODIs
71 (1988–1996), 2419 runs, (167 not out), 26 catches

I first ran into Robin Smith in 1989 in England. He made a couple of centuries against us, including 143 in the first innings of the Fourth Test, when he batted for almost a full day and the rest of his team made less than 120 between them. He was a good, tough competitor, one of those blokes that I had a few huge run-ins with on the ground and got on really well with off the ground, even though he was originally a South African. When we catch up now he doesn't hold any grudges, and I certainly don't. We both played the game the same way. We played it pretty tough, said what we said on the ground and that's where it stayed.

Robin was an outstanding batsman, although we found out in the 1993 Ashes that he did have a weakness, like most other batsmen did, and that weakness was Shane Warne! Quite simply our game plan in 1993 was, when Robin Smith came in to bat, Shane Warne warmed up.

That was the extent of our match planning against Robin. Against fast bowlers and against short bowling he had no problems. He hit the cut shot as hard as, if not harder than, any other batsman I've ever bowled to. Just smashed it. As you took the pace off the ball he struggled a bit, but against fast bowling and faster bowling, he was very good.

In the 1990/91 Ashes tour in Australia, Victoria played England at Ballarat. I made 35 not out in the first innings and in the second innings Paul Reiffel and I were putting on some runs and trying to keep England in the field so they wouldn't get a chance to beat us. At one stage Robin walked past and said to one of his teammates, 'Why does this fat prick always do well against us?'

I looked at Pistol and asked, 'Can you remember when the Ashes used to be played between Australia and England? What are you doing here, Robin?'

That was always how it was with Robin Smith. He was a combative, uncompromising competitor. That's why I respect him so much.

Ian Botham

Tests
102 (1977–1992), 5200 runs (208), 383 wickets (8 for 34), 120 catches

ODIs
116 (1976–1992), 2113 runs (79), 145 wickets (4 for 31), 36 catches

Ian Botham was one of the best all-rounders in the history of the game. Fortunately I only started playing against him towards the end of his career! In my first Test match against him at the Gabba, we had England under a little bit of pressure with two quick wickets to have them at four for 198 in the first innings. Then Gower and Botham took the game away from us. Botham got 138 and smacked the ball everywhere.

He is a gorilla of a man, just so strong. He bludgeoned the ball and you could bowl a length ball that he would block and you'd bowl the same length ball the next delivery and it would go over mid-on. The plan bowling against him was, 'I'm buggered if I know!' I didn't have too much success against him to be honest. He hit that ball as hard as anyone I played against. By the time of the 1989 Ashes tour he had lost a fair bit and he was coming back from injury. He just wasn't the same player.

He was probably the most competitive bloke of all time. He bowled medium–fast at best, but had the attitude of an extremely fast bowler. Even towards the end of his career he still had that aggression, whether it was batting or bowling or in the field. He believed that he could play himself into the game and make a difference. For a long time he did. I'm quite thankful that I never played against him in his absolute prime because we got glimpses of it in 1986/87 and he was brutal.

Michael Atherton

Tests
115 (1989–2001), 7728 runs (185 not out), 2 wickets (1 for 20), 83 catches

ODIs
54 (1990–1998), 1791 runs (127), 15 catches

Mike Atherton. God love Athers. Without trying to be critical of him, you wouldn't say he was the most naturally gifted player. But I reckon he was the most mentally tough competitor that I played against. He just loved a scrap. As a young bloke new to Test cricket, his play against us in 1989, then in Australia in 1990/91 and back in England in 1993, was exceptional. I take my hat off to Athers, he's an absolute beauty. I loved playing against him because he was always up for the contest.

But I must admit, initially I underestimated him. When I first saw Michael the words that came to mind were 'insipid' and 'scrawny'. What I saw was a university-educated young Pom, and I didn't think he would be up for the fight. When he came in against us in 1989 he just looked like a perfect target for sledging. I thought, We can get into this bloke's head. I gave him everything, physically and verbally. It was water off a duck's back. Didn't worry him. He was one of the most courageous players I've come up against. Just got in behind the ball. If every cricketer had Athers' courage and desire and discipline they would all be better players.

What's more, he used to sledge me when I would go out to bat. He would say something to me and I'd just look at him and then I'd have to ask Ian Healy, 'What's he mean by that?'

'He is probably indicating that, you know, you're a bit of a moron.'

But he was just too smart for me. His sledges were wasted on me. I read once that he was asked about my sledging of him and his reply was that he didn't understand a lot of what I said, but did know that every sledge ended in 'arsewipe'. I was trying to say 'aristocrat'. It's the worst insult I know.

Mike Gatting

Tests
79 (1978–1995), 4409 runs (207), 4 wickets (1 for 14), 59 catches

ODIs
92 (1977–1993), 2095 runs (115 not out), 10 wickets (3 for 32), 22 catches

For an Englishman, Mike Gatting is basically not a bad bloke. He was a great contributor to English cricket. The thing that I loved about him the most, though, was that he used to get some criticism about his weight and I just thought, Well, welcome to my world. It was good not to be the only one on the Test ground copping flak for that.

He was a very good player. He seemed to be very, very good against spin and the ball that Shane Warne bowled to him in 1993, the first ball that Shane bowled in a Test on English soil—'That Ball', 'The Ball of the Century', whatever you want to call it—must have put a scare through the English rooms. The ball drifted almost down leg side, pitched outside leg stump, spun back to hit the top of off stump. The margin for error in that delivery was extremely slight. If it had flicked the pad it wouldn't have been given out lbw and it wouldn't have hit the stumps. But everyone gets a good one sometimes.

He wasn't the most talented or the most graceful player but through competitive edge and desire he got a long way in his career. Over the time I played against him he had some success and I had some success against him, but it was always a battle that brought the best out of me. He was an honourable combatant.

On the ground I didn't really say much to him. He was another player who was on Allan Border's hit list, so when he would come out to bat he would be chirpy and try to have a bit of a chat with everyone, but we would ignore him to make him feel uncomfortable.

He only played one Test in the 1989 Ashes series, which was his first for 12 months. Then he didn't play another Test until 1993, being distracted by an English rebel tour to South Africa. For someone to fight their way back into any country's Test team after being dropped as captain and after one match in nearly five years is a testament to the type of bloke he was: a straightforward, straight-speaking, determined and belligerent fighter. And now that we are just two ageing codgers telling stories, he is wonderful company. No wonder I think he's a legend.

Graham Gooch

Tests
118 (1975–1995), 8900 runs (333), 23 wickets (3 for 39), 103 catches

ODIs
125 (1976–1995), 4290 runs (142), 36 wickets (3 for 19), 45 catches

For a long time I hated Graham Gooch. That probably started from when I was a seventeen-year-old net bowler at the MCG bowling to him before the 1980 Test and he just slogged me all over the place. He hit them back over my head a couple of times and in those days as a net bowler you had to go and get your own balls, so I would have to run after it, walk back, muttering, bowl, have it hit over my head again. I probably only bowled about three balls to him but every ball seemed to go for miles. I was really happy when he got run out for 99 in the first innings!

He was in Essex the year that I was there on my scholarship. So with Derek Pringle and a few of the other 2nd XI guys, I had the opportunity to play in a game with Goochie against the New Zealand touring side. I can remember the day before the game, we were in the nets. He slogged me again and I started to hate him a little bit more. That was the icing on the cake after the MCG incident a couple of years earlier. I really didn't like him.

When you play against someone, you don't really want to see their more personable side, you want to be as combative as you possibly can and not let your guard down. But when you play with someone you see another side to them. He was a great teammate, and even though I only played with him for the one game, my relationship with him became a hate/love one, because the more you get to know him, the more he grows on you, Goochie.

But my opinion of him wasn't helped by that First Test match in 1993 at Old Trafford. Mike Gatting was bowled by Shane Warne in the first innings with 'That Ball', of course, but an even more unusual thing happened in the second innings. Graham had batted really well and we had to get him out to give us a chance of rolling England and winning the match. We had them 3 for 220-odd and Graham looked like he was going to bat all day. I had been giving him plenty of short ones to duck, when I decided to surprise him by giving him a chance to use his bat. I bowled him a full-pitched one and Goochie dug it out. He hit the ball into the deck, it bounced up and looked like it was going to fall onto the stumps. He just flicked it away instinctively with his hand. I looked at Dickie Bird, the umpire, and said, 'Dickie, you can't do that?'

'Son, you're right, you can't do that.'

Out, 'handled the ball' for 133. I was really pissed off with Goochie about that. 'Handled the ball' doesn't go down as a wicket for the bowler. If he'd just let it hit the stumps, I would've averaged more than four wickets per Test match!

Goochie was a great player for England for a long time. His record against Australia would stand up pretty well, he scored a lot of runs against us at times but 1989 and 1990/91 we got a bit back on Goochie, so that was quite pleasing. He scored nearly 45,000 first-class runs and played Test cricket until he was nearly 42. Legend.

Kapil Dev

Tests
131 (1978–1994), 5248 runs (163), 434 wickets (9 for 83), 64 catches

ODIs
225 (1978–1994), 3783 runs (175 not out), 253 wickets (5 for 43), 71 catches

If he is not the best all-rounder that played world cricket he would be mighty close to it. Kapil Dev played in the age of all-rounders, at the same time as Ian Botham, Imran Khan and Richard Hadlee. He was India's best fast bowler and their best bowling all-rounder. He was declared Wisden's 'Best Indian Cricketer of the Century' ahead of Sunil Gavaskar and Sachin Tendulkar. He set the record for Test wickets at the time, passing the 431 taken by Richard Hadlee. He also led India to victory in the 1983 World Cup.

My first Test was against India and Kapil Dev. He took eight wickets. I was one of them. He had his outswinger going that day. I played and missed four balls and then nicked the fifth. Kapil was in the middle of a 21-ball spell that took 5 for 4! Having grown up on the dusty pitches in India, he developed every trick in the pace bowler's armoury as steep bounce was so rare at home. Because he was so skilful, when he came to Australia where the conditions are generally a bit better for both swing and bounce, he was sometimes unplayable. In the First Test of India's 1991/92 tour of Australia, at the Gabba, Australia had started well and we were 2 for 244 when Kapil got hold of the new ball. He served up the perfect delivery three times in a row. The experts tell me that a good batsman never gets bowled. Kapil bowled a ball that swung so late it bowled Allan Border. His next one went straight through Dean Jones, but missed pads, bat and stumps. The one after that knocked over Deano's off stump. It was a moment of magic that Dev was able to reproduce many, many times.

Kapil was one of the true gentlemen of Test cricket, and scrupulously honest. The day before the Boxing Day Test in 1985, I was inspecting the pitch with Dave Gilbert (who had played four Tests) and Bruce Reid when Kapil Dev joined us. We Aussies were having a whinge about how dry and flat the pitch was and one of us jokingly suggested that we might need to 'bend our arm' a bit to get some bounce. Suddenly Kapil's smile disappeared. Surely we weren't suggesting that we would cheat by chucking? 'No, no, no, there is no need to do that,' said Kapil. Then he beamed his huge smile and threw his arms out. 'We are all good fast bowlers here,' he said, including Dave and me, with a total of five Tests between us. 'I am sure we can all get something out of this pitch.' That was Kapil Dev. One of the greatest ever Indian players, modest about his own abilities and generous about those of everybody else.

Sachin Tendulkar

Tests
200 (1989–2013), 15,921 runs (248 not out), 46 wickets (3 for 10), 115 catches

ODIs
463 (1989–2012), 18,426 runs (200 not out), 154 wickets (5 for 32), 140 catches

The Little Master. From the day he started playing Test cricket at about eleven years old, it was clear he was going to make a lot of runs. He was actually sixteen when he made his test debut against Pakistan in November 1989. Our first look at him was when he toured Australia in 1991/92. Sachin made 148 not out in the Third Test in Sydney. On the low, slow Sydney pitch we accepted that he went well, as he was someone who grew up playing in those conditions. We had heard that he was a young star and so we weren't that surprised. Two Tests later at Perth he made 114 of India's 272 in the first innings on a very fast, bouncy pitch. He looked very comfortable, because he had such high hands and so much time. High hands let a batsman make his shot decision as late as possible and allow him to use the pace and bounce of the delivery. Tendulkar has the best hands in the game. After the Perth Test I was sitting with Steve Waugh and Ian Healy and we raised our glasses to Allan Border and told A.B. he was going to break the Test record for the most runs but warned him to enjoy it while he could because Sachin Tendulkar was going to sail right past him once A.B. retired.

He was obviously extraordinarily talented even as a young player. Speaking as a bowler, when he came in to bat, you felt like pulling a hamstring straight away. Courageous, technically as good as I have seen. An unbelievable 100 international centuries including 51 in Tests. The best batsman in my lifetime.

Mark Greatbatch

Tests

41 (1988–1996), 2021 runs (146 not out), 27 catches

ODIs

84 (1988–1996), 2206 runs (111), 35 catches

Mark Greatbatch was a woodchopper of the highest order in the top end of the New Zealand batting line-up. He hit the ball very hard and wasn't afraid to hit it in the air so on the narrow New Zealand grounds, if he got hold of you it would often carry to the boundaries. His batting reflected his attitude to the game: take the opposition on at every opportunity and don't take a backward step. Interestingly, his best innings against Australia was in a completely different style, in Perth in 1989. We batted first and made 521, with Boonie getting a double century. The Kiwis were all out in the first innings for 231 and we sent them back in, hoping to win with a day to spare. Greatbatch batted for 655 minutes and made 146 not out to save the match for New Zealand.

He had an impact on the evolution of the modern game in the 1992 World Cup where New Zealand had all their games at home. He bludgeoned the ball, showing the benefit of skilled big-hitting in the one day form of the game.

Our 1993 tour of New Zealand came down to the Third Test at Auckland, a match New Zealand had to win to retain the trophy. It was a bowler's pitch and they had to score 200 in the second innings to win, and Mark Greatbatch came out like it was a one day game. He was charging the fast bowlers and hitting us all over the place. We'd been going at it all series, I had a bit to say and he had a bit to say back, usually when we were waiting for someone to get the ball off the grandstand roof. So of course he and I had words, then we had stares, then we may have even come close to chesting each other. Unfortunately in those days they only had one or two cameras covering the game and at one point we were staring at each other and I spat on the pitch. Shot from behind me, on the television it looked as though I had dropped one pretty close to him but we were at least half a pitch length apart.

The Kiwis won the game and I can remember sitting next to Mark Greatbatch in the New Zealand rooms after the game, watching the TV news. And didn't the newsreader give it his best beating! Suggesting how much Greatbatch and Hughes must hate each other, the way that they go at it constantly, no love lost, carry on carry on. We are sitting there, looking at each other, and I agree with the newsreader, 'Yeah, pretty right, I don't like him, I wouldn't say hate, dislike immensely would be a fairer term.'

He is saying the same thing, and then the news shows the incident again. Mark turns to me and says, 'Geez big fella, if this doesn't get bums on the seats for the one dayers, nothing will!'

That's the way we both played the game. It wasn't personal. On the ground it was totally business and off the ground he was quite willing to have a beer and a laugh, and I still catch up with him when I visit New Zealand. He is a great fella.

Richard Hadlee

Tests
86 (1973–1990), 3124 runs (151 not out), 431 wickets (9 for 52), 39 catches

ODIs
115 (1973–1990), 1751 runs (79), 158 wickets (5 for 25), 27 catches

At the MCG, Bay 13 used to rip into Richard Hadlee. I reckon he would have got great pleasure from that because the Australian crowds—crowds around the world really—don't give you a hard time unless they rate you. They got into Ian Botham and they got into Richard Hadlee, so that to me is one of the biggest compliments you can get from an Australian crowd.

He was a one-man band for a long time for New Zealand. If he had played in a better team, at the pace that he bowled, he probably could have been the world's greatest first change bowler. He was one of those blokes like Terry Alderman who needed to bowl with the new ball, but he just didn't have the backup or the depth of bowling to help him out. For New Zealand to win a Test match, particularly against the stronger nations, it almost seemed that he had to take fifteen wickets a match. And you know, quite often he did that. He had good pace and good consistency. He got the ball in the right area, swung it, seamed it, cut it off the wicket. So he had all the tricks and just made the batsman play the ball. He was a very intelligent, methodical bowler.

As a batsman, he was left-handed, tough, gritty and a little bit unorthodox. He hit the ball hard and to all parts of the ground. He wasn't shy of the short stuff and was quite difficult to bowl to even though I came up against him towards the end of his career.

I played two or three series against him and you just knew what a fantastic player he was, so he was always dangerous. If he wasn't the best all-rounder in world cricket he was pretty close to it!

Danny Morrison

Tests
48 (1987–1997), 379 runs (42), 160 wickets (7 for 89), 14 catches

ODIs
96 (1987–1996), 171 runs (20 not out), 126 wickets (5 for 34), 19 catches

Like Richard Hadlee, Danny Morrison was a one-man band for a lot of the time. He came in to the Kiwi Test side at the end of Hadlee's career. If they had had those two bowlers at the same time, they would have won more Tests. Danny did a quick apprenticeship under Hadlee and then it was virtually all on his shoulders with not much support.

There was no doubting the Kiwis had a lot of guys who worked hard, but in terms of Test match–quality bowlers, they didn't have enough who consistently took wickets. Danny Morrison was a genuine strike bowler and had a bit of Jeff Thomson about his action. He was only a short guy so he had to have pace on his side, and he bowled lovely-shaped outswingers. He started on middle and off, committed the batsman to playing and then just swung away. Total effort all the time. New Zealand won only two of Danny's last 35 Tests, so it is an admirable effort for him to be so dogged a competitor in a team with that record.

As a batsman, he was hopeless! One time in Perth he was batting in the first innings of the game. Carl Rackemann was bowling to him and Danny played a beautiful forward defensive shot to a Carl Rackemann bouncer that hit him right on the badge of the helmet. It shook him up a bit. As the boys walked past we asked, 'What were you thinking?'

'I didn't expect him to bowl a bouncer!'

Dumb and brave, Danny was a genuinely skilled Test fast bowler who was totally committed to his team. Definitely not an all-rounder.

Wasim Akram

Tests
104 (1985–2002), 2898 runs (257 not out), 414 wickets (7 for 119), 44 catches

ODIs
356 (1984–2003), 3717 runs (86), 502 wickets (5 for 15), 88 catches

Wasim Akram was an amazing player. Look at his figures. He would have to be close to being one of the best all-rounders of all time. More than 400 wickets and nearly 3000 runs in Tests alone. I first came across him in Pakistan's 1989/90 tour of Australia. He was a left armer and he had a very quick action. He wasn't that big initially but he muscled up and turned into one of the world's greatest.

In that First Test he took a six for and a five for and won Man of the Match. In the Second Test he took five for 100 in the first innings, and made 52 and 123 with the bat. Won the Man of the Match award again.

Every batsman is told to watch the ball. The better batsmen watch the hand. If a bowler has an action where the batsman can see the ball during the bowler's run-up, it's easy viewing. Wasim had really quick hands and our batsmen always said it was really hard to follow so they had to pick the ball up where he released it. Wasim also bowled as quickly as anyone in the world, swung the new ball and had the great ability to reverse swing the old ball. His education under Imran Khan with the old ball would have taught him everything there is to know about reverse swing.

He is into cricket commentary now and when Pakistan is in Australia we get to hear from him. He is another admirable bloke who was highly talented and even more competitive, but knew where the boundary rope was.

Waqar Younis

Tests
87 (1989–2003), 1010 runs (45), 373 wickets (7 for 76), 18 catches

ODIs
262 (1989–2003), 969 runs (37), 416 wickets (7 for 36), 35 catches

Waqar Younis, like Akram and Tendulkar, got served up to the Australians as an eighteen year old. We first came across him in the First Test of the 1989/90 Pakistani visit to Australia, and he was a young skinny kid that had a little bit of pace. Like the other two, he became a champion.

We ran into him about two years later in some one day games, and the team meeting briefing on him was: 'A tall, skinny kid, bowls maybe high 130s at best. You're not going to be troubled by pace.' This bloke walked out and we thought, That's not the same bloke; it can't be the same bloke. He had put on about 5 stone of muscle and seemed taller too. He ran in and had the same action but bowled about 160 miles an hour quicker. This young bloke had clearly worked hard at that critical stage at the end of his growth spurt and became a huge man in a couple of years.

That day, it was a flat wicket and he bowled absolute heat. Swung the ball both ways in a one dayer.

Both Wasim and Waqar didn't really bowl a lot of short balls. Waqar was particularly good at late in-swing and he always attacked the stumps. Batsmen were more worried about getting a broken foot from his in-swinging yorker than about being hit in the ribs or in the head. I suppose that comes with bowling in Pakistan on those flat wickets. He became one of the finest exponents of fast swing bowling we have seen.

Imran Khan

Tests
88 (1971–1992), 3807 runs (136), 362 wickets (8 for 58), 28 catches

ODIs
175 (1974–1992), 3709 runs (102 not out), 182 wickets (6 for 14), 36 catches

If there is a god of eye candy in the cricketing world, it would be Imran Khan wouldn't it? He, too, cut a fair swathe through the dance floor. He was also one of the best all-rounders of his time.

I enjoyed watching him playing when I was young. By the time I got into the Australian side he was very experienced in all conditions. He was a very good swing bowler and when he was younger, he bowled good heat. He swung the ball both ways, was the father of reverse swing with the old ball and took a lot of pride in teaching others how to do it. He spent a summer playing for New South Wales and he helped Mike Whitney develop all these theories about reverse swing. Waqar Younis and Wasim Akram as young blokes coming through that Pakistan system under Imran Khan would have learnt a hell of a lot.

He was a bit of a swashbuckler when he got going with the bat. In 1989/90, the Second Test in Adelaide, we had them shot ducks. In the first innings they made about 260, we made 340. We had them three for 7 in the second innings when Imran came in. When I took my fourth wicket for the innings and sixth for the match to have them four for 22, I was thinking smorgasbord. (That's Swedish for 'back up the truck'). One more wicket and we were into the tail and I thought I would have them all out before the end of my first spell. Imran got 136 and Wasim Akram got 123. They saved the game for the Pakistanis. And this was in Imran's twentieth year as a Test player!

In the 1992 World Cup, Imran had a middling series of matches in the round robin stage but Pakistan kept winning. They chased down New Zealand's 262 in 49 overs in the semi-final in Auckland and met England in the final. Pakistan won the toss and batted at the MCG, and Imran came in with the score at one for 20. At two for 24 they were in trouble. Imran played a measured innings that always looked too slow. He had a partnership of 139 with Javed Miandad and eventually was out for 72 off 110 balls. Inzamam-ul-Haq and Wasim Akram went the tonk and set England a target of 250. Imran took the last wicket of the England innings leaving them 23 runs short and with only four deliveries left. It was the last match Imran Khan played for Pakistan.

He had a fairytale ending to a magical career. He averaged more than four wickets per Test in his 88 matches, so was a high-quality bowler in his own right. With his batting and his leadership and his Hollywood looks, he almost single-handedly popularised cricket in Pakistan.

Inzamam-ul-Haq

Tests

120 (1992–2007), 8830 runs (329), 81 catches

ODIs

378 (1991–2007), 11,739 runs (137 not out), 3 wickets, 113 catches

The thing that fascinated me about Inzy was that he not only had the slowest walk from the field—particularly if he hadn't scored many runs—but I reckon he had the slowest walk to the crease. After a wicket, everyone would be back in position, the bowler would be at the top of his mark ready to go and Inzy would be only halfway out.

He is a big bloke who hit the ball hard. He was surprisingly good against spin bowlers considering how slowly he seemed to move. Through a fifteen-year career, his record is amazing. He averaged almost 50 in Test cricket in 120 Test matches. He also took on the captaincy of an inexperienced team and got the very best out of them, including a drawn series against India and in 2005, a series victory over England, something Australia couldn't manage. When he made his 329 against New Zealand it was the tenth-highest Test score of all time.

An outstanding cricketer, who seemed to always attract criticism, but you could tell he enjoyed his cricket. Coming to the wicket, in slow motion he was going backwards, but as far as I am concerned he moved at the right pace.

Brian McMillan

Tests
38 (1992–1998), 1968 runs (113), 75 wickets (4 for 65), 49 catches

ODIs
78 (1991–1998), 841 runs (127), 70 wickets (4 for 32), 42 catches

I loved the way Brian McMillan played the game for South Africa. He's a mountain of a man and was a strong all-rounder who was very deceptive with the ball. He didn't look like he bowled all that quickly, but he was tough to face because he hit the bat so hard. He bowled just back of length and because of his strength he got a lot of bounce. He would surprise many good batsmen with his effort ball on wickets that weren't bouncing much. With the bat he was a whole-hearted performer and made handy runs. He was also a great catcher. Forty-nine catches in 38 tests is a lot for a fieldsman. He was also a very strong one-day player because of his skill set. He was considered at one stage of his career to be one of the best all-rounders in the world.

He always seemed to have a good outlook on life and a sense of humour. He didn't mind mixing it up on the field but was great company off it. One day I got a bit confused about what was on and what was off the field. The First Test of our tour to South Africa in 1994 was at Johannesburg. There had already been four One-Dayers that I hadn't played in but had been in the squad for, so I had had a few beers with some of the South Africans by then and thought Brian was a pretty good bloke. We bowled first in the First Test and I was giving Hansie Cronje a pretty hard time. He was probably their best batsman at the time and so we were targeting him. There was a bit of verbal stuff going on.

At lunch, I walked into the lunchroom, which we shared with the South Africans. I open the door and there is Hansie Cronje just standing there with Brian. 'I want to have a talk to you,' Cronje says. Brian just raises his eyebrow at me and gives me a little smirk.

I walk over to him. He's got his hands behind his back and when I'm close, he puts his arm out and he is holding the biggest handgun I have ever seen!

'Listen mate, you keep chirping on the ground, I'll bloody shoot you!' he says.

Shit, this is getting serious, I think to myself. Then they both start roaring with laughter and off they go. I'm standing there with my gums flapping and Brian looks over his shoulder with a twinkle in his eye and a big grin on his face.

After the day's play, Brian came into our rooms, gave me a beer and put his arm around my shoulders. 'How's my big tough Aussie fast bowler? Just about faints when he gets a look at a little pea-shooter! But I am pleased that it didn't stop you giving Hansie a hard time.' He apologised and said that unfortunately in South Africa guns were accepted as a part of life. Then he reassured me that if I had really pissed Hansie off, he would have pointed his elephant gun at me!

Brian averaged 39 with the bat and 33 with the ball, which qualifies him as an all-rounder. But the impact his personality had on the South African team was just as important as his numbers. He was a critical part of the re-building of South African Test cricket when the country returned to international sport. He enjoyed the game because it is a game and he made me admire all of those cricketers who make it to the top despite growing up in countries where life is less straightforward than it is in Australia. .

Kepler Wessels

Tests
40 (1982–1994), 2788 runs (179), 30 catches

ODIs
109 (1983–1994), 3367 runs (107), 18 wickets (2 for 16), 49 catches

There is only one player (other than A.B.), who played in Allan Border's first Test as captain and in his last Test as captain. Kepler Wessels! Use this information to win beer.

Kepler came to Australia from South Africa, via England, during the apartheid period, became an Australian citizen and eventually played Test cricket for Australia, before returning to South Africa to captain its Test team when it rejoined international cricket. He was in England playing county cricket when Tony Greig got him across to Australia to play and he ended up in Queensland. He was unorthodox, he looked very ugly as a batsman, but he was tough as nails. He made 162 in his first Test innings against England in Brisbane in 1982. As Clint Eastwood said, 'A good man always knows his limitations,' and Kepler knew where he was strong and what he needed to do to survive.

He was tough and he was patient and that made him a great survivor. He limited himself to no more than three shots and was a lot like Allan Border in his approach: Make runs in the areas that suit your game and don't touch anything else. He had a good defence, a good short arm jab square on the off side and he could pull the short ones. Despite these apparent limitations, he made nearly 1100 first-class runs at an average of better than 60 in 1981/82 and 1325 at 57 in 1982/83. He made nearly 25,000 first-class runs in his career. He put a very high price on his wicket and that's what made him so successful.

He was another batsman who I didn't bother sledging. Mainly because the rumour was that he was something of an amateur boxer in his younger days. So I wasn't that keen to upset him!

I remember hearing stories about a bit of high jinks that went on in the rooms, between Kepler and Rod McCurdy. Rod was a bullish, strong Victorian fast bowler who went to South Africa with a rebel tour that Kepler was on. One day Rod was getting into Kepler about his boxing prowess, he could outbox Kepler, because McCurdy had bulk and strength on his side. They put the boxing mitts on and as the story goes, Rod found out pretty quickly that knowledge, experience and guile in the boxing ring work out a lot better than brute strength. Allegedly, Kepler gave him a bit of a touch up—but that's all hearsay, I'm not sure how true it is, and every time I talk to Kepler about it he just smiles.

After he left the Australian team he played rebel cricket in South Africa and then was given the responsibility of building a South African team when they returned to Test cricket. With his class and his mental toughness he was a good choice and in a short time made South Africa a Test cricket force.

Muttiah Muralitharan

Tests

133 (1992–2010), 1261 runs (67), 800 wickets (9 for 51), 72 catches

ODIs

350 (1993–2011), 674 runs (33 not out), 534 wickets (7 for 30), 130 catches

T20Is

12 (2006–2010), 1 run, 13 wickets (3 for 29), 1 catch

I think everyone has been intrigued by him, haven't they? Does he or doesn't he? Ultimately now the rules say he doesn't. So you have to embrace what he has done for world cricket: the most Test wickets by any bowler. I think we as Australians are a little bit sour on him because he has beaten Shane Warne. But we know what a great player Shane Warne is, so for Murali to have beaten him is a phenomenal feat.

He played a couple of seasons with the Melbourne Renegades in the KFC Big Bash in 2012/13 and 2013/14 and I got to know him there. For somebody who has had such a huge impact on the game, and someone who is very, very confident in what he does, he is a surprisingly quiet presence in the change rooms—although he does have a school kid's class-clown sort of wit and sense of humour about him. He is almost like a shy school kid at the back of a meeting, too, but when asked for an opinion or for his thoughts on the game, what he delivers is superb. I suppose I shouldn't be surprised because you would expect that from someone who's played 175,000 Test matches and about 2 million one dayers, but he is a surprising bloke. You just forget that he's been around a lot and he's done a lot.

His view on the game is very simple but it's spot on. He keeps things basic. I don't like to talk about what happens within the confines of a team meeting, but in this case I'm sure Murali wouldn't mind. We were coming up against Sydney Thunder and the coach was worried about the power-hitting West Indian, Chris Gayle, and how we were going to get him out. After he asks the question in our team meeting, everyone just looks at each other because no one has a clue. When it's clear that no one else has a suggestion, Murali pipes up from the back, 'Just throw the ball to me, I'll get him out.' That's it.

'Well how are you going to do that?'

'I will bowl two offies and then I will bowl a doosra and he will be out. That's how I get him out all the time!'

On the day of the match, Gayle's at the crease and Murali comes on to bowl. He bowls him two offies and then . . . gone. What a great team plan that was!

He is an absolute ripper, Murali. I never played against him, but if I had, it would have been going over mid-wicket. Two balls in a row. Then I'd be out.

Arjuna Ranatunga

Tests
93 (1982–2000), 5105 runs (135 not out), 16 wickets (2 for 17), 47 catches

ODIs
269 (1982–1999), 7456 runs (131 not out), 79 wickets (4 for 14), 63 catches

Arjuna Ranatunga made his Test debut at eighteen in Sri Lanka's first Test appearance and was captain when they won the 1996 World Cup. He was playing for Sri Lanka at a time when Sri Lanka weren't all that good and probably shouldn't have been showing the fight that they did and he was the man who was leading the way. I was really inspired by him at times and intrigued by how tough a character he was under heavy fire.

I love the way that he played. He loved conflict, he loved the confrontation in the games and sometimes I think he incited it. He was on the front foot all the time. A lot of Australians didn't like him that much because of the way he was, and you think, Well, that's the way the Australian team is too! If he had been an Australian we would have loved him. He protected the players in a young Sri Lankan side and he took the brunt of everything. If an opponent wanted to have a crack at a Sri Lankan player, he would have to get through Arjuna first. He was a great captain and a top class batsman in both Tests and one dayers.

Chaminda Vaas

Tests
111 (1994–2009), 3089 runs (100 not out), 355 wickets (7 for 71), 31 catches

ODIs
322 (1994–2008), 2025 runs (50 not out), 400 wickets (8 for 19), 60 catches

Chaminda Vaas was an extraordinary player. Over 3000 Test runs and 300 Test wickets. Four hundred wickets in One Day Internationals. They are a legend's figures. He played for a long time and the longer he went the better he got. He isn't a big bloke and he never had any pace to lose so he always relied on control and variety, and experience gave him more of both. Change of pace, change of swing, changing from swing to cut were all tools he developed growing up in Sri Lanka on the very flat wickets there. For him to be that successful for so long using those tools in Test cricket was exceptional.

You really couldn't get after him, and the players who tried came undone. Being a left hander probably made it a little bit harder to play against him, but if you don't put it in the right spots, it doesn't matter which hand you use. Even on wickets that didn't suit him he just bowled and bowled and bowled and in a time when Sri Lanka really relied on two bowlers—him and Muralitharan—he was outstanding.

Viv Richards

Tests	
121 (1974–1991), 8540 runs (291), 32 wickets (2 for 17), 122 catches	

ODIs	
187 (1975–1991), 6721 runs (189 not out), 118 wickets (6 for 41), 100 catches	

Viv Richards. He was an intimidating, imposing man. He was so strong from the shoulders to the waist. He was just a V of massive proportions, and such a hard hitter of the ball. I was once asked how tall he was and I have memories of him as 6 foot 2 or thereabouts. He is 5 foot 10.

Bowling to him, you knew that if you weren't quite right he was going to hit you. Everyone can remember his pulling and his hooking. He wasn't intimidated by the short ball and his driving was better than Jack Brabham's.

He was so difficult to bowl to because he could create his own lines. You would be bowling to him wondering where he was going to hit you. You would try to bowl a length ball at off stump and he'd be backing away hitting you over cover, or he would be hitting you straight down the ground and the next ball, same spot and he would step across his stumps and put you behind square leg.

I still remember him playing shots in a one dayer in Sydney where he was hitting Greg Matthews over mid-wicket with one hand. One-handed shots. Normally if a hand comes off the bat it lofts the ball, so the first time his hand came off the cry went up, 'Catch it!' and it was ten rows back.

We were at Perth one day and I had been hit for four. The West Indies were none out for plenty. Tony Dodemaide picked the ball up out of the gutter, jogged back, threw it to me and said, 'C'mon big fella, get a wicket.'

'Why?'

'That's what fast bowlers do.'

'Mate, we've got Gordon Greenidge and Desmond Haynes batting now. If I get a wicket, Richie Richardson comes in. Then if I get another wicket, Viv Richards comes in. I need some encouragement, Dod.'

How did I bowl to him? Very carefully. He was on his way to 151 in Perth in 1988/89 and we got a wicket at the other end. The team was in a huddle and Tony Dodemaide came up from fine leg and said there was a bloke on the boundary who reckoned he knew Viv Richards' weakness: kryptonite. Too right.

Towards the end of his career, he became even harder to bowl to. He didn't need to make big hundreds to justify his place, so he made it his responsibility to set games up. Then he would go on a rampage, because he didn't care if he was dismissed, he just wanted to score quick runs. And sledging him was pointless because it just made him go harder.

He was brutal, as was his approach to his captaincy, which involved a constant onslaught of pressure on the opposition, whether they were batting or bowling. I think he inherited that strategy from Clive Lloyd, and applied it just as effectively. It was a big part of the extended period of dominance by the West Indians. The West Indian attack was intimidating, but there wasn't anything more intimidating as an inexperienced bowler than having Viv Richards at the other end, bat in hand.

Gordon Greenidge and Desmond Haynes

GORDON GREENIDGE

Tests

108 (1974–1991), 7558 runs (226), 96 catches

ODIs

128 (1975–1991), 5134 runs (133 not out), 1 wicket (1 for 21), 45 catches

DESMOND HAYNES

Tests

116 (1978–1994), 7487 runs (184), 1 wicket (1 for 2), 65 catches

ODIs

238 (1978–1994), 8648 runs (152 not out), 59 catches

These two opening batsmen made sixteen century stands in Tests and four of those scored more than 200 runs. They were the greatest opening partnership Test cricket has seen and need to be thought about as a partnership. I started watching them as I was getting into cricket, and saw what a fantastic coupling they were.

By the time I started playing they had been around for a long time and they were supremely confident, and knew each other's game tremendously well—and that's exactly what you don't want from an opening pair if you are bowling to it! I soon discovered that their partnership also had several other dimensions to it that made them an awesome challenge. One of the challenges for a bowler was that you couldn't identify one as the aggressor. From innings to innings and game to game they would exchange roles of aggressor and stonewaller. If one got off to a bit of a flyer the other would just hang around and occasionally they would both go.

The problem with that was that early in the Test match when you would be trying to take wickets, you would want to back off the aggressor and focus on the guy that was being more defensive. The principle was to attack the defensive one, because if you attack a bloke that's attacking it can backfire on you. With players as talented as Greenidge and Haynes, that was only going to end in tears for the bowler. So basically, you just had to be careful of them both.

Secondly, most batsmen can be identified as either length players or line players. Line players are front foot players, where if you bowl wide of the stumps, they will let it go. The length players will play all the shots and they are more likely to be back foot players. Once you understand a player's style you can make plans according to that. With Greenidge and Haynes, as well as seeming to take random turns in being aggressive and defensive, they were confusing as opponents because they both had the ability to be both line and length players. Both showed the full face of the bat. Sometimes they wouldn't cut, they wouldn't play the short ball, and other times they would. So just when you thought after a couple of Test matches you had them sorted out, and you'd develop a plan accordingly, things would change and you'd be left floundering.

So they could make fundamental changes to their individual style of play, and transform themselves from innings to innings. I'm not sure if it was by design or just by the way they felt on a particular day. But they were both extraordinary players, and in combination they were the best cricket has ever seen.

Richie Richardson

Tests
86 (1983–1995), 5949 runs (194), 90 catches

ODIs
224 (1983–1996), 6248 runs (122), 1 wicket (1 for 4), 75 catches

Richie's performance, against all comers, was unbelievable. For a long time there he played fourth fiddle to Gordon Greenidge, Desmond Haynes and Viv Richards. You could easily think that he hooked and cut and pulled for a living but he could also make runs against good spin bowlers, which is a sign of a great player. He kept his best for Australia and scored nine centuries against us; more than anyone in the modern era except Sachin Tendulkar.

Richie is the player that I dismissed more than anyone else in my Test career. His approach to batting probably forced me to bowl well to him. If I bowled too many short balls to him I would get bored because they would take a long, long time to be retrieved. So I'd try not to bowl short to him and then he would just clobber me off the front foot!

When I first played against him I suppose we had no plan for him because we were more worried about Greenidge,

Haynes and Richards. But the whole West Indian top four was awesome. If you got through that you were really excited because it wasn't often you got through those four guys. They were so good they were intimidating with the bat.

The thing that amazed me most about these players was that off the ground, they are a great bunch of blokes. They were ruthless on the ground and fantastic company off it. Richie was a gentle, friendly, intelligent man who took over the captaincy of the West Indies when Viv and Gordon and Desmond left. That was a monumental task and I think took a toll on his performance but in his prime he was one of the most magnificent batsmen I ever played against.

Brian Lara

Tests
131 (1990–2006), 11,953 runs (400 not out), 164 catches

ODIs
299 (1990–2007), 10,405 runs (169), 4 wickets (2 for 5), 120 catches

Brian Lara had to work hard to get a regular spot in the West Indian Test team. Given the batsmen that were in the team, that is not surprising, but it was well known what a great player he was. He played a single Test in Pakistan at the end of 1990, then played a one-off Test against South Africa in April 1992. We toured the Windies in 1991, and he wasn't in the Test team but we played a tour match against him and you could tell then what a great player he was going to be. But I don't think anyone knew he was to become one of the all-time greats of the game.

In the 1992/93 series at home against the West Indies, we discovered Brian Lara. In his fifth Test match, he made 277 at the SCG. It was an exceptional innings and he went on to make runs against every attack in every Test venue, against all bowlers in all conditions. He was left-handed free-flowing with a big backswing. He was magic to watch.

In the 1999 Australian tour to the West Indies, I was lucky enough to see him get 150 without having to bowl to him. The West Indies were chasing 308 to win the Third Test at Bridgetown. Lara came in at three for 78. On a fifth-day wicket, nine times out of ten you would expect Australia to win, especially with an attack of Glenn McGrath, Jason Gillespie, Shane Warne and Stuart MacGill. At tea, the Windies were eight for 254. Brian Lara had to make 150 to win the game and he did. That to me is a sign of a true champion. I put that down as the best Test innings that I've watched.

Technically he was very good because he had a great defence. His big backswing made you think you may be able to get under him with yorkers. But he had extremely quick hands and his decision-making was very good. It is unbelievably hard to bowl to a bloke who can hit you anywhere around the ground off either the front foot or back foot, and he had that ability. When a bowler is working over a batsman, often the objective is to vary the length within a narrow margin to try to get the batsman undecided about what length to play. There are a lot of players you can get caught in between front and back foot, but you could never beat Brian Lara for pace and because he was so clear-minded and decisive, you rarely caught him in the middle ground.

I didn't have too much to do with him off the ground, but everything that I did showed that he was a great bloke. For a long time he would have had the weight of the world on his shoulders every time he went out to bat; if he failed the West Indies failed. But he loved the game, and he was a truly humble champion. Just a West Indian kid having a great time playing cricket. He was an extraordinary, outstanding talent.

Malcolm Marshall

Tests
81 (1978–1991), 1810 runs (92), 376 wickets (7 for 22), 25 catches

ODIs
136 (1980–1992), 955 runs (66), 157 wickets (4 for 18), 15 catches

There was not much of Malcolm Marshall, he was less than 6 foot tall, but he was a nasty man with a cricket ball in his hand. Ran in fast and bowled fast. Viv Richards only used him sparingly. Used the young blokes like Curtly Ambrose, Courtney Walsh and Patrick Patterson to do the hard work and if he needed someone to break a partnership, Malcolm would come on and just bowl his five or six overs and bowl them very fast. He's the quickest bowler that I ever faced and his was a really uncomfortable kind of quick. If he wanted to hit you, he hit you. He swung it both ways in all conditions. He averaged more than four and a half wickets per Test, so he was as potent as Glenn McGrath He was an outstanding bowler.

Then off the ground, he was as meek and mild a bloke as you'd ever meet. He always seemed to have a smile on his face. I suppose if you played in the West Indian side in the late eighties and early nineties and bowled as fast as he did you probably didn't have too much to worry about.

Curtly Ambrose

Tests
98 (1988–2000), 1439 runs (53), 405 wickets (8 for 45), 18 catches

ODIs
176 (1988–2000), 639 runs (31 not out), 225 wickets (5 for 17), 45 catches

Curtly Ambrose, the silent assassin. He didn't say much and some could get the inkling that he was arrogant but he just liked keeping to himself. One night Tim May, Steve Waugh, Ian Healy and I bailed him up at a function in the West Indies in 1991. We pretty much cornered him so he couldn't get out (given that he was 6 foot 7, it was going to take all four of us to stop him from leaving if he really wanted to) and we were pumping him full of questions. He's a friendly, shy bloke with a real love for the game.

He wasn't as imposing as Joel Garner because he was at least an inch shorter. His build was more like Glenn McGrath's too and he bowled a lot like Glenn. Smooth, efficient action, very consistent and always putting the ball in the right spot. Because of his height, the bounce of the ball helped him so he could bowl a good length ball that would hit you in the ribs. He wasn't just speed and bounce either, he was a very skilful cricketer and could use the seam as well as anyone. His record speaks for itself.

To face him was very awkward because he never gave you too much to hit and never, never said too much, never. I think I only saw him once get upset and a bit steamy. That was against Steve Waugh in the West Indies. The classic irresistible force and immovable object. There is a famous photo of Richie Richardson pulling him away from Steve. If Richie hadn't stepped in, the pair of them would still be standing staring at each other. It was so rare to see Ambrose actually losing his cool. Normally, he just ran in and bowled. Hardly spoke; all his intimidation was through his actions. Oh yeah. Not a fun bloke to bat against.

I have caught up with Curtly since our playing days. We had him and Richie Richardson in Antigua to speak to spectator tours that I host. At one of these nights, I heard that as a young bloke he'd had an offer to play basketball in America. He confirmed that was right; he'd had to choose between that and cricket. Why did he choose cricket? 'My mum wanted me to play cricket and you do what your mum tells you.' So he is scared of his mum!

Courtney Walsh

Tests

132 (1984–2001), 936 runs (30 not out), 519 wickets (7 for 37), 29 catches

ODIs

205 (1985–2000), 321 runs (30), 227 wickets (5 for 1), 27 catches

Courtney Walsh was an incredible bowler who stood the test of time. Courtney is another tall bloke who had an efficient action and who used his height to extract bounce. He had endurance, he had strength. If you look at the West Indies line-up you would never say that he was the best bowler, but he saw off a fair number of his teammates. In the early part of his career he was rarely the leading bowler, so most of his overs were into the wind in support of Malcolm Marshall, Curtly Ambrose, Patrick Patterson, and then a little bit later, Ian Bishop. But Courtney just hung in there, and like Glenn McGrath, he bowled and bowled and bowled, and he bowled for a length of time that fast bowlers aren't supposed to be able to manage! He played Test cricket for close to seventeen years and 132 Test matches, but he played first-class cricket for Jamaica and Gloucestershire as well, so he didn't rust between Test matches. A total of 429 first-class matches and 1807 wickets, plus another 778 wickets in one day games, international and domestic! He is the new W.G. Grace. He was 38 when he played his last Test. That is an unbelievable feat for a fast bowler.

He built his skills and broadened his game so at the end of his career he had all the tricks. By this time the West Indies had lost their dominance, and it was Walsh, Ambrose and Brian Lara who were really holding the West Indian side together.

As a group, the West Indian fast bowling attack was awesome and they dominated Test cricket throughout my career. But most of them were pretty hopeless with the bat. At one stage, Courtney held the Test record with 43 ducks. Initially, the Australian Fast Bowlers Cartel had the view that if we didn't go too hard at the body when we were bowling to them, we might live through our batting innings. Look after them and they'll look after us. But on the 1988/89 tour by the West Indies to Australia, Clive Lloyd was the West Indian team manager. Clive had developed the four fast bowlers strategy after being clobbered by Lillee and Thomson. I am not sure if it was a coincidence, but it became quite apparent pretty early in that tour that it was every man for himself. Walsh, Ambrose, Marshall and Patterson had a very simple game plan: bowl out the top seven and kill the bottom four, and I was part of that bottom four. It wasn't much fun.

At that time helmets and chest pads and arm pads were being developed. There was more protection, you really couldn't get hurt. Unless you were Geoff Lawson and got a broken jaw, but he didn't have a grille on his helmet. Once that happened, in the Second Test at Perth, all bets were off. Their strategy was obvious, so we had nothing to lose by trying to bounce them.

That sounded like a brave strategy, until I got to the Fifth Test at Adelaide. We won the toss and batted. Dean Jones was having one of his days and was heading for a double century. I batted for a long time, I got 72 not out and I reckon I got hit more times than I got runs. I had deep-seated bruising in both shoulders and on my chest from Marshall, Patterson, Walsh and Ambrose. I copped an absolute barrage. But my teammates gave me all the support they could. At the Adelaide Oval the players' viewing rooms were square of the wicket and on a relatively narrow ground with the windows open, from time to time you can hear the encouragement that they might shout to you. It became quite apparent that my Australian teammates were really enjoying my innings. Every time I got hit, there was always a bit of an ooh sound from the crowd, but the noise coming from the players' area was different. It sounded a bit more like laughter. I would look up and none of the boys seemed to be looking at me so I assumed that their amusement was being caused by something else. Then about fifteen seconds later there would be another big roar of laughter. I couldn't work out what was going on; I assumed someone was playing up and having a joke about something. After about five or six overs of this laughter and then an echo of it shortly after, the pennies had dropped. Watching me get hit live was giving them a laugh. Watching me get hit on the replay made them laugh even louder. So that's the type of teammates I had in the Australian side!

Out on the ground, I think the West Indians might have been enjoying it a bit too, although they weren't saying anything. In fact, I can't remember ever being sledged by a West Indian bowler. They were bowling *to* Dean Jones and bowling *at* me and that's it. They were working me over, just systematically working as a team of bowlers. I learnt a lot that day in the middle. Malcolm Marshall was getting to the end of his career so Patrick Patterson was doing a lot of the grunt work, running in and bowling fast. I worked out that they bowled the young blokes, then when Viv wanted something done he would bring Malcolm back. Malcolm was the quickest bowler I faced and he just toyed with me. If he wanted to hit me, he'd hit me. I don't think it was too much of a challenge after a while.

We took a lot of lessons from that series by watching how the West Indies went about it. At this stage our team was still very much in development. Watching the West Indians helped us develop the strategies that A.B., Tubby, Steve Waugh and Ricky Ponting used to get Australia to the top. You go hard at the opposing captain and you try to break him, and then you give the bottom four everything you've got. If the bottom four make 50 or 60 runs, the tail's wagged, and it may be the difference in a Test match. The West Indians planted the seed that they didn't want us to be out there, and that when we came out to bat, they were going to hurt us. That's exactly what happened.

During the First Test against the West Indies in Jamaica in 1991, before we went out to bat, Allan Border turned around and he went through the batting order. 'Everyone knows what the order is: Geoff Marsh, Mark Taylor, Boonie and me, then Dean Jones, Mark Waugh, Greg Matthews and Heals.' Mike Whitney, Craig McDermott and I looked at him, waiting for the rest of the order. He looked at us and said, 'Toss a coin, it doesn't matter!' It was harsh but it was fair in hindsight. Six for 357. All out 371. So he was right. It really didn't matter.

Occasionally, they did help us out though. In 1991 in Guyana, both teams were staying in the same hotel and the night before the first day's play we had to walk about 800 metres down the road to a pub. We were going there for our team meeting and the boys who organised it got into a little bit of trouble because we were having the team meeting at the same venue as the West Indian team! As we were leaving the hotel, Tim May, Steve Waugh, Ian Healy and I saw Curtly Ambrose, Patrick Patterson and Courtney Walsh in the foyer.

We told them where we were heading and they asked us to wait so they could walk down with us. We declined but Courtney insisted quite firmly, 'No, no, seriously, you must wait.'

A couple of minutes later we walked out of the hotel and I asked Courtney if there was a problem. He looked at Patrick, who looked down at his hand. There was a Crocodile Dundee, 'That's not a knife, this is a knife,' scenario going on up his sleeve. I looked at Heals, a bit worried now, and asked what was going on. Walsh said, 'You just might need it in Guyana.' As a group, the West Indian fast bowling squad was a terrifying prospect through the eighties and nineties. They were a physically intimidating bunch, but when it really counted, they knew cricket is just a game.

DECLARATION

Many people have helped me give this account of my legends of the game. Claire Kingston and Sue Hines have shown the patience of openers on a green Gabba pitch. Angela Handley and Clare James have performed with aplomb. Many thanks to Alexia Pettenon. Thanks to Sam Giannopoulos for taking me on and for his support and advice. Thanks to Peta and Gary for putting up with me trying to bowl left-handed in the backyard. Most of all, thank you Sue, Maddy, Tim and Scott for everything.

I have used a number of sources for this book. Jack Pollard's *The Complete Illustrated History of Australian Cricket* continues to stand the test of time. *Encyclopedia of Australian Cricket Players* by Ken Piesse and Charles Davis is a wonderful publication, and www.espncricinfo.com is a detailed and authoritative source. I have checked details as closely as possible. Any errors are Thommo's.

ABOUT MERV . . .

Merv Hughes made his Test debut in 1985 against India. He took one for 123 and made a duck. Surprisingly, he went on to play 53 Tests and 33 one-day internationals for Australia. In the Test arena, Merv took 212 wickets and scored 1032 runs, becoming the third Australian to take more than 200 wickets and make more than 1000 runs. He joined Ray Lindwall and Richie Benaud with that feat. When he retired, he was the tenth most successful Australian wicket taker in the history of the game.

He played all of his Tests with Allan Border as captain. In 1988/89 against the West Indies he took eight wickets in the second innings and thirteen wickets for the match. He was a member of the 1989 Ashes team that regained the Ashes in England for the first time since 1934. After the end of his playing career, he served as a national selector during Australia's latest rebuilding phase.

104 LEGENDS

Harry Alexander   111

Curtly Ambrose   263

Warwick Armstrong   24

Michael Atherton   210

Peter Bedford   184

David Boon   3

Allan Border   43

Ian Botham   208

James Brayshaw   176

Ray Bright   47

Ian Callen   171

Greg Campbell   62

Ian Chappell   115

Michael Clarke   99

Gary Cosier   181

Jamie Cox   178

Colin Croft   129

Alan Davidson   196

Tony Dodemaide   36

Ken Eastwood   157

Steven Feltsted   153

Damien Fleming   104

Sam Gannon   122

Joel Garner   126

Mike Gatting   212

Ron Gaunt   155

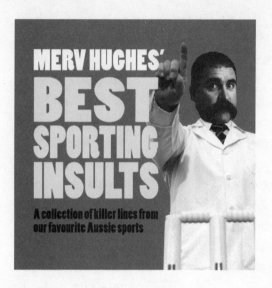

Australian sportsmen are known worldwide for their
hilarious and, quite frankly, inspired sledges. Over the years,
there have been some classic lines uttered on a variety of
sporting fields and arenas, whether it's across the cricket pitch
or on the footy field.

Merv Hughes' Best Sporting Insults is the ultimate collection
of sporting insults, brought together by a man with a
reputation for his humorous witticisms and cutting sledges.

Paperback: ISBN 978 1 74237 519 9
Also available as an ebook: ISBN 978 1 74269 206 7